THE
COMPLIANCE
FORMULA

Successful Strategies Of CMMC
Compliant Companies

Published by TechnologyPress™, Lake Mary, FL.

TechnologyPress™ is a registered trademark.

Printed in the United States of America.

ISBN: 979-8-9862097-2-2
LCCN: 2022919535

This publication is designed to provide accurate and authoritative information with regard to the subject matter covered. It is sold with the understanding that the publisher is not engaged in rendering legal, accounting, or other professional advice. If legal advice or other expert assistance is required, the services of a competent professional should be sought. The opinions expressed by the authors in this book are not endorsed by TechnologyPress™ and are the sole responsibility of the author rendering the opinion.

Most TechnologyPress™ titles are available at special quantity discounts for bulk purchases for sales promotions, premiums, fundraising, and educational use. Special versions or book excerpts can also be created to fit specific needs.

For more information, please write:

TechnologyPress™
3415 W. Lake Mary Blvd. #950370
Lake Mary, FL 32746
or call 1.877.261.4930

THE
COMPLIANCE
FORMULA

Successful Strategies Of CMMC
Compliant Companies

TechnologyPress™
Lake Mary, Florida

CONTENTS

CHAPTER 1

WHY ACT NOW? WHAT CMMC REALLY MEANS AND HOW TO USE IT TO GAIN A COMPETITIVE ADVANTAGE

BY STUART BRYAN

Don't wait.

If you are a contractor in the Department of Defense supply chain, whether you interact with the DoD exclusively or are a subcontractor, or if you are a Managed Services Provider providing IT support to a manufacturing defense contractor, you have an obstacle to overcome and overcome relatively quickly.

In the near future, Cybersecurity Maturity Model Certification (CMMC) 2.0 Level 1 or 2 will be necessary for any organization that creates or handles in any way Controlled Unclassified Information (CUI) and/or Federal Contract Information (FCI).

Let me emphasize, this isn't just for DoD contractors. Companies up and down the supply chain are starting to require cybersecurity assurances.

I've spent two decades in IT and am in the compliance trenches following CMMC developments daily, so I can tell you that if you've been lulled into thinking these requirements won't pertain to you or that you have plenty of time, think again. This could put you way behind – or even eliminate you from the bidding process. In extreme cases, it could mean facing business closure.

Before I get into the background of CMMC and how it will benefit you beyond just winning contracts, it's helpful to understand why there is such urgency for CMMC compliance.

WHAT'S THE HURRY?

US information networks are targets of cyber-attacks every day, and cyberthreats continue to evolve. The Defense Industrial Base (DIB) is a prominent target for cyber-attacks, which are becoming ever more frequent and complex.

Over the last 25 years, China has become a much larger player on the world stage, with advanced manufacturing facilities, well-trained engineers, and scientists. Plus, there are state-sponsored efforts to exfiltrate data from Western nations' data centers and infrastructure, and this player has a blatant disregard for international copyright and patent law. Additionally, Russia has been an aggressor on the world stage since Vladimir Putin took office, and he has clearly set his sights on restoring Russia's supremacy as a great power on the international scene.

The rapid advancement of China's military and technological prowess has partially come by way of espionage and interfering in offshore manufacturing by the US and other countries. With the push for dominance on a global stage, as well as steadily expanding its reach and influence throughout the Pacific, it's increasingly clear to US officials that China's ambitions represent a clear and present danger.

HOW WE GOT HERE

In 2002, when Windows XP was still the new operating-system kid on the block, the Federal Information Security Modernization Act was passed, empowering the National Institute of Standards and Technology to set national standards for cybersecurity. NIST standards have provided the foundational building blocks for most of the regulatory compliance requirements in place in the US today. Requirements such as the Health Insurance Portability and Accountability Act (HIPAA), for example, are based on NIST standards.

The primary goals of these standards are to define how data is stored, transmitted and accessed. They include both physical and logical controls. For example, under HIPAA, when protected data is displayed on a computer monitor, it must be shielded from outside direct sightlines with a physical screen protector while requiring that the same data be stored logically encrypted if it is mobile in any way, such as on a tablet, laptop, flash drive or e-mail.

The aim of the CMMC program is to prevent FCI and CUI from being released publicly. Whether under intentional, accidental, or malicious circumstances, you and the DoD don't want this information to fall into the wrong hands.

All DoD contractors and subcontractors must comply with the Federal Acquisition Regulation FAR and the Defense Acquisition Regulation Supplemental (DFARS). In 2017, to aid in these efforts and to secure the DIB, a specific set of controls published under NIST SP-800-171 provided guidance to all DoD contractors who were subject to DFARS 252.204-7012, so they could self-access these controls. But because this was a self-assessment, not every organization or its IT provider interpreted and applied the control framework correctly or accurately. Additionally, it was dependent on the organization's ability to state alignment and compliance with no independent assessment by any qualified organization or individual. The problem: simply stating that one is compliant does not make it a factual statement.

Sadly, this allowed the Chinese military to steal F-35 Lightning II joint strike fighter plans as far back as 2009. They did this not through a spy stealing the master set of plans but through cyber-espionage techniques across a multitude of attacks on small DoD contractors. The bits and pieces stolen from these contractors in and of themselves would not be helpful to the Chinese at all. But once they got enough pieces, they were able to stitch them together. In 2012, the Chinese military flew the J-31, a near-copycat of the F-35, for the first time. The continuing challenge is to stay one design cycle ahead of other countries because it takes 10 years from concept to completion. This cyber-espionage caused the US to lose that 10-year advantage.

After this, the DoD created CMMC to speed up compliance and require validation of compliance, not just self-attestation. It was the theft of CUI that was the actual issue in the case of the F-35/J-31.

WHY IT'S CRITICAL TO KEEP INFORMATION SAFE NO MATTER WHAT

Intellectual property (IP) must be closely guarded by every organization. While Top Secret and CUI are even more critical to protect, most companies in the US DoD supply chain and the DIB won't ever handle or even create Top Secret information. They do, however, routinely handle, store, and transmit CUI and FCI. When interested parties like the Chinese Communist Party in the People's Republic of China are willing to go to extraordinary lengths to access and collect that data, it's critical to our nation's defensive capabilities that this information is kept safe. With technologies like widespread 5G mobile broadband and gigabit (and faster) wired broadband speeds, the time it takes to exfiltrate large amounts of data has dramatically decreased, making it even easier to steal data.

One area that often gets overlooked is the need to protect your own company's intellectual property. A local company – which, for privacy reasons, I won't name – had an engineer swipe their design by copying documents onto personal storage and taking them to a competitor, who hired them. The competitor then took the design to market first, which resulted in lost contracts for the company that did the original design work. Had this company had CMMC standards in place, it would have helped guard their company's IP.

In your organization, you must be aware that while perhaps you don't have Top Secret information, you do have IP that must be guarded. If you lose that information, you could end up wasting money on developing products and lose your competitive advantage or your ability to market effectively if someone can do it cheaper, faster, or easier.

These factors combine to create an immediate need to enforce higher standards of data security. One that cannot and will not be ignored. This reason alone would be enough to push for rapid implementation and enforcement of CMMC standards.

OTHER WAYS COMPLIANCE WILL PROTECT YOU AND YOUR PROFITS

Our mission at I-M Technology, LLC, is to make compliance a competitive advantage for the clients we serve. While there are clear reasons to be concerned about making the changes both physically, procedurally, and structurally to achieve CMMC compliance, from the perspective of an IT professional with over 20 years of experience with small and medium businesses, I can confidently say these changes will benefit your business.

When my company onboards a new client, we always ask for their employee onboarding and offboarding processes. This provides a clear indicator of the level of operational maturity they have and a predictor of their willingness to adopt better cybersecurity and technology management standards. No one likes to show up on their first day of work to a computer that's not set up, with no access and permissions granted or programs ready but no training program in place to follow. However, put in the reverse, it's terrifying to think that there's no process to quickly eliminate any individual's access to programs, data, resources, or IP.

Getting CMMC compliant gives you the established processes, procedures, and standards. It defines the who, the what and the how of your organizational systems and automatically makes your organization more process-driven. It removes doubt and variability. Plus, it can and should help you scale and scale more effectively.

One of our clients came to us with an extremely disorganized network. They had a mishmash of technology and used inefficient, antiquated processes. Plus, they had employees wasting their skills doing manual data entry tasks that could be performed faster and more accurately with technology. By putting this framework in place, they became more operationally mature. Employees enjoy their work more now because they do more meaningful work. Plus, as a result of getting their organization in shape, they scaled the company 300% and were acquired.

I can tell you from direct experience that people appreciate well-run, technologically current, and competent organizations that keep an eye on ways to help them be more productive and keep their jobs safe. When staff struggle with disorganized, disjointed systems and processes, they can see when problems with the process are being solved with payroll. Meaningless, needless, or mindlessly repetitive tasks are done because someone didn't think it through and ask why and how to make it better. Organizations like the one I described above most often grow organically, and that leads to inherent messiness. The work to get CMMC compliant provides a fantastic reset button. It will drive much of that out of your business and lead you to evaluate and perhaps validate that the appropriate systems are in place to succeed. HR, finance, IT, and operations will all have to be involved as you move toward the level that is right for what you handle. The good news is that with the right people and the right partners, you should find the right tools to assist with this journey.

CMMC 2.0 MEANT TO SIMPLIFY THE PROGRAM

Concerns about CMMC range from the expense to the difficulty of implementation. It's important to understand that the DoD doesn't want you to go out of business or drop out of the DIB. They want you in there but keeping critical data safe.

CMMC is still based on NIST SP-800-171. However, CMMC 2.0 collapses the original cybersecurity framework from five levels to three and removes all CMMC unique practices and processes, which simplifies the program for both contractors and the DoD. We'll break all this down for you in layman's terms in the chapters ahead.

WHY IT'S A MISTAKE TO TAKE THE HEAD-IN-THE-SAND APPROACH

Sadly, too many of the DIB contractors I've met over the years since 2017 chose to wait to comply until they were forced to do so or believed that somehow they'd get an exemption due to sole source rules. This is not the case. Recently, I met with a DIB contractor who told me he refused to comply with CMMC because he was the only one who could make what he was providing. As it turns out, he's not the only one in the world. If the other company complies with CMMC standards, who do you think the US government is going to choose?

As I write this chapter in October 2022, there are primes (top-level DIB contractors) requiring attestation to DFARS NIST 800-171r2/CMMC Level 3 standards. Businesses are having to fill out Supplier Performance Risk System scores that can determine whether or not they get awarded or keep their contracts. I've personally assisted clients with this process and seen the communications from primes to their subcontractors informing them that they must at least self-attest to DFARS NIST 800-171 standards. Choosing to not do this will have direct financial implications for your company.

There is no way to ignore this unless your organization is willing to cease being part of the federal supply chain. That is, in fact, occurring and, frankly, depending on what percentage of revenue the DoD-related work produces, it might be the best approach fiscally for you. The good news is that this opens the likelihood for increased opportunities and makes a compelling argument for getting your company CMMC compliant instead. As the estimated timeline for getting compliant is 12 to 18 months, there's no better time to get started than right now.

LIMIT EXPOSURE WHILE MAKING THE PROCESS SIMPLER

We've established that CMMC can help you:

- Keep our country and your company safe.
- Make your company more operationally mature.
- Scale more effectively.
- Give yourself a competitive advantage.
- Win (and keep) DoD contracts.

As you evaluate your company's specific situation, it's important to restrict the scope of the systems and people that will handle, in any way, CUI and/or FCI to limit your financial exposure. The simpler you can keep the scope of this, the easier it is to manage. When exploring this, I highly recommend working with a Certified CMMC Practitioner, as they have gone through the necessary training and had that training validated.

A word of caution here. Some vendors, advisors and consultants take the heavy-handed approach as their first and perhaps only recommendation. It's the difference between the carpet-bombing in World War II and the tactical strikes possible today. There's simply no need for solutions that are wider in scope and cost than they need to be. If you're concerned that you can't afford to get CMMC compliant, the primes can and will help, and costs can be covered through federal programs.

For many companies, it will be possible to take the enclave approach where some IT systems and people can be designated as those that will handle CUI and/or FCI. For others, the conclusion will be that it doesn't make sense to have that segregation and will make the entire company system greater in scope. Neither approach is more correct than the other.

I simply encourage company leadership to look at the cost operationally and financially to both. The chapters in this book will help you do this and greatly simplify the process. Getting CMMC compliant in a financially and operationally sustainable way will give you a competitive advantage when you go after contracts. If you can deliver lower-cost outcomes based on your better implementation, then your offering will be more attractive. That should help you win more contracts. And that benefits your company and your people and helps retain profits.

In any case, the reality is that it takes a sustained team effort from a combination of IT and cybersecurity professionals, internal HR, finance, and operations staff to properly implement the controls found in CMMC. But don't give up. The rewards are better on the other side.

Sources:
- https://www.washingtonpost.com/world/national-security/a-list-of-the-us-weapons-designs-and-technologies-compromised-by-hackers/2013/05/27/a95b2b12-c483-11e2-9fe2-6ee52d0eb7c1_story.html
- https://www.defenseone.com/threats/2015/09/more-questions-f-35-after-new-specs-chinas-copycat/121859/

About Stuart

"Technology has the almost magical ability of unlocking the potential in people by getting rid of mindless, repetitive tasks that can make our lives less meaningful."

Stuart Bryan is the Co-founder and President of I-M Technology. With over 20 years' experience, he is passionate about helping small and medium businesses grow by removing constraints and bottlenecks that stop or slow down production while also allowing people to focus on the work that is meaningful to them.

On his path to better himself, a series of work experiences provided the background for how he thinks about and approaches business today. From observing meaningless jobs that could be replaced with technology to seeing how inefficiencies can destroy even the largest companies, Stuart took these life experiences and designed intelligent processes that would help him and his clients improve their quality of life – while helping their businesses thrive and grow.

Eventually working for a large computer company, he discovered that a well-run IT Department can provide a competitive advantage for a business and really help it grow. But after this large company went out of business due to overdependence on a single client, combined with inefficiencies and lack of processes, he was determined to prevent other companies from suffering a similar fate. It was out of the ashes of this former employer that Stuart cofounded I-M Technology, LLC, with his father, Phil Bryan, in 2003.

With a broad base of knowledge in the areas of networking and computer software and hardware, Stuart set out to help businesses set up intelligent, proactive processes that would help them grow. He also supports his clients with technology that comes alongside what they do, giving them the ability to focus on the products and services they deliver. This allows them to scale their company while spending more time focusing on their strengths and doing what they enjoy most.

Today I-M Technology has grown to provide services to organizations dealing with compliance requirements based on NIST standards such as 800-171 DFARS and now CMMC 2.0. Preferring to be strategic and offer right-sized solutions that protect profits and productivity, Stuart and his team help businesses comply with changing regulations in a way that is cost-effective and smartly applied. Their mission at I-M Technology is to make compliance a competitive advantage for the clients they serve.

As a Managed Services Provider, I-M Technology has a holistic view of technology in the modern office and endeavors to take the headache out of IT. Approaching problems from a business perspective, they find ways to leverage technology to make their clients' staff more productive and connected.

Continuing to do meaningful work and improve lives, Stuart serves as a mentor to IT leaders around the English-speaking world. He's been featured in national IT publications and been a guest speaker on podcasts and at national industry events.

Get in touch with Stuart:
- Email: sbryan@i-mtechnology.com
- Phone: 866-755-4486
- https://www.i-mtechnology.com/

CHAPTER 2

THE GOVERNMENT DOESN'T CARE THAT YOU DIDN'T KNOW

HOW TO PROTECT YOURSELF FROM PAYING FINES AND GOING TO JAIL IF YOU GET HACKED (WHO'S LIABLE?)

BY ADAM CROSSLEY,
CEO – Fairoaks IT

It just doesn't seem fair. Owning a small business is one of the toughest responsibilities today. You have to constantly juggle multiple important functions: Sales. Marketing. Operations. Administration. Accounting. Human Resources. On top of all those priorities, you are also responsible for satisfying your customers' needs, bringing in revenue to make payroll and being profitable so your family can thrive. And if you really want to be successful, you can kiss the 40-hour workweek goodbye. Working nights, weekends and holidays becomes the norm.

As if those responsibilities weren't difficult enough to navigate, cybercrime today has made it considerably more difficult to run a business. First, there's the real threat of getting hacked and having your data stolen and encrypted until you pay an exorbitant payout. Second, once word spreads you had a data breach, especially if it involved your customers' private data, you'll experience a PR nightmare that will cost you current and future customers.

But there's also a third risk that affects millions of small businesses today. It's a risk that, if left ignored, could seriously impact you with lost business opportunities, fines and, yes, even jail time. Yet, on the flipside, when you fully understand and comply, it can actually become a very lucrative opportunity for your business!

Here's the problem: far too many small business owners today are completely unaware that this risk even exists. That's why I wanted to better educate small business owners about this very real risk, as well as about the opportunities it may present if you take the appropriate actions.

THE OFTEN-OVERLOOKED IMPORTANCE OF CYBERSECURITY COMPLIANCE FOR GOVERNMENT CONTRACTORS

While your local CPA firm, attorney and chiropractor must deal with the real risks of cybercrime, all government contractors must also navigate the strict waters of cybersecurity compliance. Since the goal is to reduce risks to national security, the Department of Defense (DoD) has created a compliance model to raise the level of information security across the entire Defense Industrial Base. This compliance measure is known as the Cybersecurity Maturity Model Certification, or CMMC.

It's important to note that anyone who sells to the US government, no matter how insignificant the sale may seem, is responsible for following the government's CMMC compliance standards. Naturally, giant global contractors, such as Lockheed Martin and Northrop Grumman Corporation, must follow the government's CMMC standards. But the standards also apply to the three-person family business making subcomponents and shipping them off to a prime defense contractor such as General Dynamics. Yes, that business is still liable for all the rules and regulations of CMMC, because that subcomponent may eventually outfit a nuclear submarine. That business must follow the exact same criteria that a Lockheed Martin would.

This is the point that too many small business defense contractors don't fully understand. In the eyes of the government, small mom-and-pop businesses that supply the government must operate under the same CMMC guidelines as the major players. No one is exempt.

HOW CMMC COMPLIANCE COULD COST YOUR BUSINESS SIGNIFICANTLY (OR POSSIBLY MAKE YOU WEALTHY)

Today, all Department of Defense contractors, including the subprime contractors, are required to register with the Supplier Performance Risk System, or SPRS. That is the authoritative source to retrieve supplier and product performance information assessments for the defense acquisition community. The government uses this resource to identify, assess and monitor unclassified performance.

So, any business that provides anything to the DoD must register as a supplier on the SPRS website to show they are following CMMC compliance regulations. Therefore, if you fail to disclose your compliance on this site, your business won't be listed to bid on any government projects. Suddenly, Lockheed Martin is no longer calling on you to supply them with your products. Money talks. So, for most business owners who sell to the DoD and its prime contractors, this is the reason they eventually get their ducks in a row and choose to become CMMC compliant – neglecting compliance regulations could cost them considerable revenue through lost contracts.

Because the government is cracking down on businesses that

don't prove their cybersecurity compliance by submitting to the SPRS, the pool of competition for suppliers is shrinking. Many small business owners simply aren't aware of the new regulations or don't know how to become compliant. That's an opportunity for you! When your business is one of the few contractors that the government deems in compliance, you can bid on and win more projects. In other words, becoming CMMC compliant will not only bolster your cybersecurity to protect you from a data breach or ransomware, it could pay off in the long run with considerably more revenue.

UNDERSTANDING THE RISKS OF COMPLIANCE NEGLIGENCE

The more that small business owners realize they will no longer be able to bid on government contracts if they are not CMMC compliant, the more likely they'll take action. Unfortunately, if they don't have anyone in IT, as well as someone to act as a compliance officer, too often they'll just wing it. To them, the SPRS comes across as a compliance survey. So, they fill it out to the best of their ability and score themselves on their level of compliance.

If that's the case, here are a couple of scenarios. In one scenario, where they are as honest as possible, their business is still listed as a contractor because they submitted their compliance. However, because their compliancy score was weak, the likelihood they'll win many projects is pretty low. Lockheed Martin and Boeing are likely to pass them by in search of a vendor that offers stronger cybersecurity and compliance regulations.

In another scenario, they simply don't know what they don't know. One question on the compliance survey may ask if they have an access control system for their building. The business owner answers "yes" because they have a standard lock on the door. However, they don't realize that by "access control," the CMMC compliance officer actually means a keycard system to track who is coming and going, etc. Sure, the business may initially win a contract. However, when the CMMC compliance auditor comes knocking next year and realizes they were not forthright, the business will lose the bid. Even worse, if the auditor believes the business has falsified these compliance documents, it's punishable up to the level of treason. That's because, whether it was intentional or not, you have defrauded the US government. As a result, you could face serious fines or even jail time.

Ignorance of the law or of compliance regulations is not an excuse. It doesn't matter if you are a one-person shop. It doesn't matter if you don't have an IT services provider or internal IT person. It doesn't matter if you know nothing about compliance, CMMC and the SPRS. It's the government. And they want everyone following their rules, or you assume the consequences.

It's all about what risk level you are comfortable with. By not addressing cybersecurity, you put your network, your customers' information and your business at serious risk. By ignoring the compliance requirements from the government, you risk losing lucrative contracts and the high-profit revenue that comes with them.

WHO'S LIABLE FOR THE FINES, PENALTIES AND POSSIBLE JAIL TIME?

The question on most business owners' minds: Who's actually liable if you neglect your compliance regulations or falsify them? First, the company is certainly liable financially. From a personal perspective, all the documentation and attestations need to be signed off on by a particular individual at your company. That's usually a chief information officer, chief information security officer or compliance officer.

With my personal experience in past positions of dealing with International Traffic in Arms Regulations, the government can also target the business executives, such as company presidents, vice presidents and the CEO. While they may not be as close to cybersecurity and compliance as an IT manager, they are ultimately responsible for what's going on in their company and what they're committing to.

Therefore, if you do supply the government and you neglect to meet their standards of cybersecurity, compliance and reporting, any or all of these positions in your company can be held liable. Ultimately, any of those positions could be responsible for paying fines or even serving jail time.

PREDICTING THE FUTURE OF GOVERNMENT-MANDATED CYBERSECURITY COMPLIANCE

Consider how widespread cybercrime and ransomware attacks have become today. They're everywhere, and they're bringing small and large businesses to their knees. In response, government-mandated cybersecurity compliance will only grow, in my opinion.

The Defense Contract Management Agency employs people who travel to defense manufacturing facilities to monitor their processes. The DCMA auditor will inspect the facility and interview the staff to make sure they are running their organization exactly the way the government expects. I believe that because the DCMA already has people out there at defense contractors and manufacturers, this agency will take over the responsibility of auditing cybersecurity compliance.

At a Cybersecurity Maturity Model Certification Accreditation Body town hall meeting in 2022, a DCMA representative announced that the agency will begin assessing contractors' compliance against the NIST 800-171 security controls through the "Medium Assessment" process that the DoD prescribed in the interim rule that created Defense Federal Acquisition Regulation Supplement 252.204-7020. In a Medium Assessment, the government reviews the contractor's current documentation, including the System Security Plan and the contractor's previous self-assessment, which contractors were required to complete by November 2020. It was mentioned at the meeting that these assessments would start soon.

Because cybercrime is getting more attention, I expect there will be a lot more government audits and scrutiny in the near future. That means there will be a lot more auditors going after smaller businesses. It also means you can expect more scrutiny and more fines and penalties if you're not following the CMMC framework.

THE ANSWER TO PROTECTING YOURSELF AND YOUR BUSINESS

You just learned about all the fines and penalties that could be forced upon you for not employing sufficient cybersecurity measures and following the CMMC guidelines. That doesn't even include all the lost opportunities to bid on projects.

Unfortunately, far too many small business owners who supply the Department of Defense falsely believe they can handle all of this on their own. Most business owners fail to realize that meeting the CMMC guidelines is a massive undertaking involving immense time, effort and expense. The basis of CMMC is a special publication titled National Institute of Standards and Technology (NIST) 800-171. A few years back, the government issued a study where they determined the average cost for a company to become CMMC compliant was close to $200,000! To save time and money, you need IT experts and compliance officers in your corner.

Fairoaks IT uses NIST 800-171 as a cybersecurity framework not only for our clients, but also internally for our own MSP business. This robust measure of cybersecurity protections consists of more than 100 controls that apply to protecting "Controlled Unclassified Information" at defense contractors. However, because we take security so seriously, we follow many of the same controls ourselves.

In addition, Fairoaks IT offers a Compliance Security package for clients needing to be compliant with any government or insurance regulation, including CMMC. For our clients, we can become their virtual CSO, or chief security officer. To meet the CMMC requirement, we hold semiannual executive briefings for our clients where we ensure that the SPRS survey is completed to the government's standards and our client is tracking to complete any actions identified within the Plan of Action and Milestones. Not only do we ensure this critical survey is accurate, we save our clients considerable time and headaches by taking care of the reports and creating points of action and milestones to complete.

While you may consider following the CMMC cybersecurity guidelines to avoid fines, penalties and even jail time, enacting these higher measures of security benefits your business in multiple ways. You'll be far less likely to endure the massive expense, sales-sinking downtime and PR nightmare that you could experience after a hacker encrypts your files and demands a hefty ransom. Also, because you'll be listed as a prime vendor to bid on government contracts, you'll likely have more opportunities, revenue and profits.

BEYOND SECURITY, FAIROAKS IT FOCUSES ON SERVING OUR CUSTOMERS

Since we have been leading IT support consultants since 1991 – over 30 years – we have built the business around a few core tenets that serve our valued customers. These core tenets guide our decision-making and actions every single day.

EDUCATION comes first. Education is vital throughout our organization. Naturally, to better educate our clients, we must sufficiently educate our entire team. Therefore, if an employee comes to us and wants to get a new certification or get trained on the latest cybersecurity software, we pay for it and get it done on company time. No questions asked.

Doing it RIGHT the first time. Doing it quickly doesn't mean you're going to get it right. Often quick work simply gets you to a new problem even faster. For that reason, one of our core tenets is to really take the time to get it right the first time.

Our view is that we aren't simply fixing the problem at hand. We DISSECT the problem, determine WHY it happened and figure out how to best SOLVE it and prevent it from ever happening again.

We treat your business just as we treat our own. It's the golden rule: treat others the way you wish to be treated. At Fairoaks IT, the products and services we recommend to keep your network and computers secure are the EXACT ones we implement in our own cybersecurity environment. This also means we will only recommend services and solutions that are aligned with your budget rather than suggest a spaceship-sized server for a three-person accounting firm.

THE GOVERNMENT AND FAIROAKS IT SHARE A COMMON GOAL: TO PROTECT YOUR BUSINESS

A decade ago, the government didn't have all these cybersecurity regulations and mandates. But back then, our biggest cyber concerns were spam and annoying adware. With the proliferation of cyber-attacks and ransomware that can cost business owners millions of dollars, the government was forced to step in.

Today, government suppliers are having to warm up to the idea of strict compliance regulations. But rather than think of it as extra reporting and paperwork, think of it as their efforts to help protect your business.

That's what the government and Fairoaks IT have in common. Our business was built on the goal of protecting small businesses like yours from cyber-attacks and ransomware. That's why we provide a robust cybersecurity stack that follows the government's

CMMC guidelines. That's why we work closely with your team to help you navigate the complex and ever-changing world of cybersecurity compliance. That's why small businesses have counted on Fairoaks IT for over 30 years!

About Adam

Adam Crossley is CEO of Fairoaks IT, a cybersecurity and managed services provider with locations in Charlotte, NC, and Franklin, MA. Adam brings together his vast experience in cybersecurity, IT management and process improvement, and applies it to affording his clients with enterprise-level IT security and support.

Having worked in the defense manufacturing industry – most notably for Sikorsky Aircraft on the US Navy's Seahawk helicopter program – Adam knows what mission critical means, and he's able to bring that same level of focus to his clients' IT and cybersecurity needs. Today, Adam uses those same skill sets to ensure that more than 1,200 users across 60 clients are optimized for productivity while keeping them compliant with NIST 800-171 and CMMC standards. He has also coordinated cybersecurity incident responses large and small, and helped numerous clients win more government contracts by getting them compliant.

When Adam isn't helping clients who have benefited from Fairoaks IT's services for 10, 20 or even 30 years, you'll usually find him outdoors, flying or traveling. But there's nothing he enjoys more than spending time with his caring wife, Kimberly, and their two young boys, Theodore and Harrison.

Get in touch with Adam:
- Email: adam@fairoaksit.com
- Web: https://www.FairoaksIT.com

CHAPTER 3

MANAGING RISK: EVALUATION CRITERIA FOR SELECTING AN IT PROVIDER

BY ARTHUR LEIBY,
President – The Lerepco IT Group

Choosing an IT services provider 20 years ago wasn't too difficult. Most of them utilized similar tools to fix PCs when they went down. The main differentiators were the people – their responsiveness and level of service. You could essentially throw a dart, and you would most likely find a pretty good IT provider.

Fast-forward a few years, and these IT services providers moved from a reactive stance of fixing broken computers to a proactive position of monitoring and prevention. Now called managed services providers, these MSPs ensured that networks and computers were always up and running to keep companies productive. Some had better tools than others. Some had better service and more experienced technicians than others, but signing on with most any of them would usually improve your efficiency.

While a fast and efficient network is certainly still important, today it's also imperative to have dependable cybersecurity tools and strategies to protect your network and data. Without a doubt, the exponential surge of cybercrime and the potential for losing millions of dollars from a single ransomware attack have forced MSPs to quickly rachet up their cybersecurity skill sets and tools. Here are a few reasons why MSPs today are becoming far more security-focused:

- By 2025, Cybersecurity Ventures predicts ransomware will cost $10.5 trillion annually.
- 52% of businesses struck by a ransomware attack reported suffering over $500,000 in damages. (Source: NinjaOne)
- Ransomware remediation costs organizations more than $1.4 million on average. (Source: Sophos)
- Gas shortages across the US were felt after the nation's largest fuel pipeline, Colonial Pipeline, was hacked. The cyberthieves stole 100 GB of data in just two hours and demanded $2.3 million.
- The world's largest meat supplier was forced to halt operations even after it paid $11 million to regain access to confidential files after a cyber-attack.
- The Baltimore city government was hit with a massive ransomware attack that left it crippled for over a month and cost it $18 million.

Make no mistake, when evaluating which IT provider or MSP to put your trust in, it's all about managing risk. Sure, everybody who works on computers today will tell you they handle cybersecurity. But do they truly have the expertise, the tools, and the strategies in place to minimize your exposure? And in the event you are hacked, do they know how to jump into action to get you back up and running with minimum downtime and financial loss?

Frankly, it's hard to know. Too many small businesses think their network and data are protected from cybercrime – until it happens to them. That's why I wrote this chapter. I want to make clear what you should look for in an MSP and cybersecurity team today. I also want to share the questions you should ask any prospective IT provider so you can be confident you ultimately choose the right one to best manage your risk.

I. A SOUND BACKUP AND DISASTER RECOVERY SOLUTION IS PARAMOUNT

It's just a normal Friday at your business. But just minutes earlier, one of your employees accidentally clicked a malicious link. Now you're staring at a message on your monitor that sends shivers down your spine:

**"Your computer has been locked.
All of your files have been encrypted."**

It goes on to explain that the only way to get access to your computer, work files and client records is to pay in Bitcoin, which equals several hundred thousand dollars! You quickly learn that every computer in your office has the same ominous message. Your business is dead in the water. No sales. No revenue coming in. No work being done. And this could last for days or even weeks.

Now you're looking at paying out hundreds of thousands of dollars, losing many clients, destroying your reputation, and facing the possibility of lawsuits and fines. At this point, your only way out of this nightmare is to have a dependable backup. If you do, while it can still be a headache for your business and take time to sort out what data is affected, it's nowhere near the nightmare you would experience if you didn't have that backup available. By having a trusted backup, there's no ransom payment...no significant downtime...no lost customers, damaged reputation or lawsuits.

That's why when you're considering an IT provider, here are two of the first questions you should ask them:

1. **Can you provide a timeline of how long it will take to get my network back up and running in the event of a cyber-attack or disaster?**

2. **Do you INSIST on doing periodic test restores of my**

backups to make sure the data is not corrupt and could be restored in the event of a disaster?

Notice how you're not simply asking, "Do you have a backup and disaster recovery plan?" It's important to be very specific, because the future of your business could be at stake.

Years ago, I asked a potential medical-group client if he had sufficient backups for all their patient records and if they tested those backups. He assured me that his former IT guy had taken care of that. Then, the very day they signed on with us, someone had clicked on an email link, and a ransomware attack encrypted all their files!

Believing their former IT company did what they said they were doing, we tried to restore their backup files. They all failed! None of their backed-up data could be restored because their previous IT consultant never properly tested their backups. As a result, this medical group had to pay to get the key, enabling decryption of all the data files that were encrypted.

This is why it's absolutely imperative that your IT provider or MSP test your backups on a regular basis. Because without a recent backup of your data, you could be on the hook for a massive payout, not to mention a substantial loss of productivity, considerable time lost and a PR nightmare that could cost you customers.

At the Lerepco IT Group of Moorestown, NJ, our data backup solutions automatically perform a complete system backup as often as every half hour! In addition to continuously having your backup files tested, you should demand a complete image backup from a virtual or offsite server. An old-school backup to tape does you no good if the server catches fire or is stolen. Besides, tape backups do eventually fail.

Consider it your "get out of jail free" card. Having proven and tested backup systems and a disaster recovery plan in place will significantly minimize your lost time, headaches, and expense if a hacker breaches your network. Failure to have a proven backup plan in place could bring your business to a screeching halt.

II. YOUR FIRST LINE OF DEFENSE: YOUR TEAM

Once you are confident your IT provider has a proven backup and disaster recovery solution, you should focus on preventing the cyber-attack in the first place. And that starts with training. While it's the hackers who ultimately deliver the malware and ransomware, all too often it's the employees who unintentionally open the door for them.

These recent statistics can't be ignored:

- Around 90% of all data breaches today originated from phishing. (Source: IBM)
- About 15 BILLION spam emails are sent every single day.
- In 2022, six BILLION phishing attacks are expected to occur.

That's why managing your risk must start with training your entire team. That includes both phishing simulations as well as cybersecurity training. Too many IT providers take a hands-off approach to education and training. Either they abdicate that responsibility to their clients, or they simply 'dump' educational materials on them that rarely get read and implemented.

Here is what you should ask a prospective IT provider to ensure they provide the necessary education and training that can help prevent a data breach or ransomware event:

◆ **Does your team provide ONGOING cybersecurity education to my ENTIRE team, including phishing simulations?**

◆ **Do you provide formalized cybersecurity training that's**

monitored for completion as well as testing of the course material?

At the Lerepco IT Group, we insist on providing both phishing simulations and cybersecurity training for all our clients. We conduct at least one phishing simulation a month via video that is tied directly to the business vertical. For example, doctors and attorneys are more likely to click on a link if it comes from LinkedIn.

From these harmless phishing simulations, we always review the results and let the clients know which of their employees opened the email and clicked on the link or attachment and who may have gone so far as entering their private information. These results are shared in monthly meetings so corrective action can take place.

We've seen firsthand how these phishing simulations bolster clients' cybersecurity. When we first send out the phishing emails, it's crazy how many employees click the links. After a few months, practically nobody clicks the links. Suddenly, that business's risk of suffering a cyber-attack diminishes substantially!

Beyond phishing simulations, we regularly provide comprehensive cybersecurity training videos to all our clients' end-users. For example, effective password management is one of those trainings. We teach clients how to use a longer string of characters that are not sequential, including numbers and symbols, rather than simple passwords that can be easily stolen and sold on the Dark Web.

Remember, it may be the hacker who emails the dangerous link to your team, but it's typically a team member who clicks that link to wreak tons of havoc throughout your organization. Don't let it get to that point. Manage your risks by finding an IT provider who provides thorough and ongoing cybersecurity training and phishing simulations.

III. LOCKING DOWN YOUR COMPUTERS TO PROTECT YOUR NETWORK AND DATA

Once you believe you've sufficiently managed your risks by considering an MSP that values ongoing training as well as maintaining and testing backups, your next question should be:

- **What tools and strategies do you use to lock down our employees' PCs and devices to ensure they're not compromising our network?**

If your prospective IT provider simply answers, "Antivirus software," or "A firewall," take caution. They're operating from an early-2000s perspective. Today, you need a whole arsenal of specific tools and strategies to foil the world's most sophisticated cybercriminals.

Cybersecurity today must take a layered approach. It starts with a robust firewall that's designed to protect your network and data in today's remote working environment. Your firewall should guard against malware and viruses while offering threat protection in terms of downloading files.

Today, using an old-fashioned antivirus simply isn't good enough. You also need an endpoint detection and response (EDR) tool that automatically monitors threats on all of your endpoints 24/7. The more sophisticated tools provide detection, investigation, threat hunting and even response capabilities. In other words, you're taking a very proactive approach to cybersecurity rather than waiting for a cyber-attack.

In addition to a proven firewall solution and EDR tools, multifactor authentication (also called two-factor authentication) is an absolute necessity nowadays to shut down cyberthreats. Multifactor authentication requires a computer or network user to provide two or more verification factors to gain access to an application, online account, or VPN. Rather than achieve instant access when a username and password are entered, MFA may also send a code to the user's phone or require fingerprint verification.

Another layer in this vast web of cybersecurity is DNS filtering. This is especially important today, when so many employees are working remotely with laptops. They go from their hotel room to their homes to the local coffee shop and can pick up any virus from the free Wi-Fi or from suspect websites. DNS filtering simply blocks malicious or forbidden websites and applications at the DNS level so they can't be loaded on user devices.

You can rest assured that the Lerepco IT Group applies a layered approach to cybersecurity, including all these tools and security measures, to successfully lock down all of our clients' computers and networks. In addition, we strongly encourage our clients to consider purchasing a cybersecurity insurance policy. That way, in the rare event they do face a cyberthreat or ransomware attack, the insurance company will assist with the investigation, provide a complete PR team, and even pay the ransom amount. Now, that's peace of mind!

IV. ADDITIONAL CONSIDERATIONS WHEN CHOOSING AN IT PROVIDER

While cybersecurity is a top priority in managing your risk when choosing an IT provider, you also want to select an MSP that puts their clients first. Of course, EVERY MSP will tell you they value their customers. *But do they truly?*

Here's a quick way to check their level of customer service – call them! That's right, with a quick phone call, you'll know how much they care about their customers. Do they expect you to leave a voicemail, which may mean days before getting a return call? Do they have an automated attendant, which feels cold and impersonal? Do they outsource their support team to a foreign country? Or does their team member answer their phones LIVE?

At the Lerepco IT Group, we answer every call LIVE! We do this so we can better listen to your IT issues and even solve your problem in real time. Our clients love this difference.

Second, does the IT provider you're considering want to be a strategic partner in your business? *While most business owners view their IT company as an expense, we prefer to be seen as an investment...an asset.* At the Lerepco IT Group, we want to have open communication and quarterly meetings with our clients to discuss their current needs, objectives, and any foreseeable problems.

Most of our clients couldn't run their business without technology. Therefore, IT is a strategic part of their business and needs to be treated as such. Our clients see us as their CIO or virtual CIO.

V. WHICH IT PROVIDER WILL MINIMIZE YOUR CYBERSECURITY RISKS?

Ask peer business owners who endured the massive costs, disruptive downtime, customer loss and humiliating results of a cyber-attack, what would they have done differently? I guarantee you, ALL of them would have done their homework when it came to hiring their IT provider or MSP. They would have asked better questions. They would have asked for testimonials and even client references. They would have scrutinized the company's experience, their cybersecurity stack and even their strategies.

While no IT provider can guarantee you won't be hit with a cyber-attack (and if they do guarantee it, RUN because they are lying), the Lerepco IT Group provides a multilayered approach to cybersecurity. Our cybersecurity stack is powered by artificial intelligence and machine-learning and encompasses all the protections discussed in this chapter. But don't take our word for it, just ask our valued clients. Many of them we've been working with for 10, 15 and even 20 years!

About Arthur

Perhaps Arthur Leiby's early life became a lesson that taught him how to best serve multiple-location businesses. Long before Microsoft was a household name, Art was building custom applications at AT&T, the originators of the UNIX operating system.

In 1993, Art started a company creating custom software for newspapers with two friends: a fellow graduate of Moravian University who worked with him at AT&T, as well as another AT&T co-worker. Because owning a business often pulled him away from his family, Art sold his business interest in 1999 to be a better dad.

Art's career then led him to help a lifelong friend grow his value-added reseller (VAR) business. Figuring he would be there for a year or two, Art proved his loyalty by gaining software and hardware expertise for a decade and a half!

Together with his good friend Bob Puphal, Art founded the Lerepco IT Group in January 2014. "I always knew I would start my own business again. I just didn't know it would take 15 years to get there," Art says.

To his business, Art brought decades of experience in working with large companies such as AT&T, Verizon, Lucent, and Sodexo. He always knew he could introduce enterprise-level tools and technology to attorneys, engineers, medical teams, and other small businesses in the New Jersey area.

From the start, Art set up his business to better serve his clients. Rather than the typical MSP, they call their business a managed IT department (MID), which means they act as their clients' IT department without nickel-and-diming them to death.

The Lerepco IT Group's specialty is working with multilocation-type businesses. Whether he's working with attorneys, engineers or medical teams, Art helps integrate satellite offices with seamless communications through site-to-site VPN connectivity and cloud-based technology.

Living in Mount Laurel with his wife and three children, Art has been a part of the South New Jersey community for most of his life. Along with providing exceptional service to his clientele, his Jersey lifestyle is one of Art's top passions.

Contact Art here:
- Web: https://www.lerepco.com
- Phone: 856-206-5600
- LinkedIn: https://www.linkedin.com/in/artleiby

CHAPTER 4

HOW TO BECOME CMMC COMPLIANT

WITHOUT BUSTING YOUR BUDGET (OR YOUR BRAIN)

BY GREG ZIMMERLE,
Founder & CEO – myIT.com

A client called me recently, frustrated because they lost a vital customer contract. Their customer – a Department of Defense supplier – called my client to say, "All our subcontractors must have CMMC compliance. Are you certified?" At the time, my client was not compliant because they didn't know they needed to meet basic Cybersecurity Maturity Model Certificate (CMMC) requirements to be a subcontractor of a DoD supplier. Unfortunately, my client lost that contract. That's why they called me with questions like: Will this keep happening? Can I afford CMMC compliance? Where do I even start?

I've been in the technology industry for three decades and I am the CEO of myIT.com for 25 years. I'm not sure I know of a process that involves more acronyms than CMMC. There are NIST, RPOs, C3PAOs, CUI, FCI…and the list goes on. CMMC changed the way my business works too. When the DoD released

CMMC 1.0 in 2020, we had to learn the ins and outs of CMMC to help our clients understand the process and what they must protect themselves against. In the tech industry, we're constantly adapting to the latest breach with software updates and employee training. It's ongoing work. It's constant work. We've built processes around it and got it down to a science.

As a 30-year veteran of the technology industry and a CMMC Registered Practitioner (RP) and Registered Practitioner Organization (RPO), I answer questions every day from my clients. Here are my answers:

- Yes, you will keep losing contracts for DoD contracts without compliance.
- Yes, you can afford it by tailoring a budgeted timeline (usually six to 12 months; up to two years) to your goals.
- You start right here by understanding the value of CMMC for your future business growth.

WHAT YOU NEED TO KNOW: CMMC IS THE NEW SECURITY STANDARD

Here's what I tell my clients they need to know (hint: it's not the acronyms):

CMMC standards for security are the new foundation of the security industry. CMMC compliance includes cybersecurity and physical security; it's every security angle for a business. While it's only required for companies that are prime or subcontractors or suppliers to the DoD, it outlines the basic standards every company should be using to protect their information.

You may think you can lose one or two customers who contract with the DoD. The problem is that it's not just the federal government requiring basic security standards to do business. Cybersecurity insurance companies, state governments[1] and other private bodies

---

1. https://www.ncsl.org/research/telecommunications-and-information-technology/cybersecurity-legislation-2021.aspx

are creating their own security standards, following trends within the security industry. From 2020 to 2021, cyber-attacks increased by 31%, according to Accenture's State of Cybersecurity Report in 2021.[2] There are more cyber-attacks and breaches today than ever before, and they are increasing in frequency and severity, so organizations are acting. I still hear clients say, "But who would want to attack a plywood manufacturer? I'm no one compared to these big companies!" Cybercriminals know that the further down the supply chain they hunt, the weaker the security is. That's why successful organizational breaches via the supply chain increased from 44% to 61% from 2020 to 2021. Everyone is fair game to cybercriminals.

If you fail to become CMMC compliant, you may risk losing insurance and put your company at a greater security risk. You'll continue to lose out on bids for contracts. In a few years, your growth will stall. The stakes are higher every day, and the burden of constantly adapting to new security standards lays the pressure on thick for business owners.

As an RP and RPO, I consult my clients on how to break down the CMMC process into manageable steps that align with their budgets and goals. When you go through the process, you'll likely find that many controls are already in place! For those that aren't, the key to CMMC compliance is taking one step at a time. You identify the controls you need, then apply your available budget along an implementation timeline. That's how you become compliant without breaking your brain or busting your budget.

HOW TO BECOME CMMC COMPLIANT WITHOUT BUSTING YOUR BUDGET (OR YOUR BRAIN)

Many business owners have handled their own security for a long time, and it's largely worked – until now. Recently, the owner of an $80 million-a-year company reached out to me.

2. https://www.accenture.com/_acnmedia/PDF-165/Accenture-State-Of-Cybersecurity-2021.pdf

He'd been doing his own IT for over 10 years. When he received a cybersecurity checklist from his insurance company, he realized he needed to prove he had basic cybersecurity hygiene and become CMMC compliant. He called me and said, "I can set up a computer and connect it to a network, but I can't do this. It scares me that I don't know if I am secure or not. If I do this on my own, I'll never know if I'm doing it right."

Many of us are comfortable sticking to what we know, but CMMC isn't the same as connecting to a network or installing a firewall. It's a lot more than that. My prospect acknowledged that and chose to work with a CMMC expert so he could trust it was done right. He kept his insurance policy without hefty premiums and could continue landing major contracts. He achieved every control he needed over a budgeted timeline without stalling his work. Whether you're an $80 million company or a $1 million company, you can too.

CMMC 1.0 VS. CMMC 2.0: A PRIMER

There are two versions of CMMC: CMMC 1.0 and CMMC 2.0. CMMC 1.0 is a five-level model released in 2020. CMMC 2.0 is just like it sounds, an improved version of 1.0. CMMC 2.0 is a three-level model; the initial framework was released in 2021 but is not expected to go into full effect until late 2023. CMMC 2.0 replaces 1.0, whose requirements have been suspended.

What you need to know: CMMC 2.0 is what any company will use when seeking to start the certification for the first time. It has three levels of certification: 1, 2 and 3. These levels build on one another, from foundational to expert-level requirements. Many of my clients are Level 1 or Level 2.

Level 1 (Foundational): Includes 17 basic standards (also called controls or practices) met through an annual self-assessment. This level applies to companies that handle Federal Contract Information (FCI), which is information provided by the government that's not for public release.

Level 2 (Advanced): Includes 110 advanced standards aligned with NIST 800-171 (requirements for protecting CUI – Controlled Unclassified Information). These standards require a third-party assessment and handle CUI, a.k.a. sensitive information that requires additional safeguarding compared to FCI.

Level 3 (Expert): Includes 110+ standards based on NIST 800-172 (additional requirements to protect CUI) that require triannual government-led assessments. This applies to a smaller number of companies working with CUI on the DoD's highest priority programs.

FOUR STEPS TO CMMC COMPLIANCE

As I've said, CMMC affects every department in your business, not just technology. The first step is to bring your executive team, especially your IT professional, preferably an RPO, to the table. Together, it would be best if you decided which level (1, 2 or 3) is appropriate for your business. If you host this conversation off the bat, you will save your brain hours of frustration and endless discussions about standards and the compliance process. Get everyone to the table so you are all on the same page. Then you can follow four steps to streamline your CMMC compliance within budget:

1. **Assemble your team and choose the appropriate level.**
2. **Download the audit checklist and review it with your team.**
3. **Conduct a gap analysis.**
4. **Create a road map that outlines which standards you need to prioritize and realistically budget those deadlines.**

The nice thing about the process is that it doesn't have to happen all at once. Most of my clients are CMMC compliant in six to 12 months. After their gap analysis, they know what standards they are missing. Then they can prioritize which to work toward, based on their budget. They can adjust their business process to include the new standards over time; that's how you avoid breaking your budget. Now let's look at each step more closely:

1. **Assemble your team and choose a CMMC level.**
   The best way to decide which level is right for you is to start by calling your clients. Ask:

   - Do you contract with the DoD?
   - Are you Level 1, 2 or 3?

   This will help you determine if the basics in Level 1 are enough or if you need more advanced certification, like 2 or 3. It comes down to how sensitive the data is that you are handling.

   Then get your team together to review the standards for your level. Your team will need to include you and department heads, the person in charge of physical security and your IT professional – whether they are internal or outsourced doesn't matter. If you have a virtual CIO or virtual CSO, loop them in. If they aren't well-versed in CMMC, you need to bring someone on board, like an RP/RPO, who is. This will make the process much easier! Again, our goal is to make this as easy as possible.

2. **Do an initial assessment with CMMC best practices.**
   Each CMMC level has its assessment you can do online at https://www.projectspectrum.io/.[3] You will need to register a free account to access the assessments and training.

   No matter what level you decide on, you still must complete the one(s) before it. If you are working toward Level 2, you still must complete Level 1 because they build off each other. If you are working toward Level 3, you must first become certified in 1 and 2. The good news is that if you've been keeping up with basic cybersecurity, you will find that you already have many of the controls in place for Level 1 or even Level 2. All you need to do is verify them.

---

3. https://projectspectrum.io/

3. Conduct a gap analysis.

The gap analysis is just that: it reveals the gaps in your current process by comparing what you do have marked off on your checklist to what is yet to be completed. Some of the practices you need to hit might be behavioral, like adding a sign-in sheet to your front desk to monitor guest activity while in your building, or they might be more advanced, like replacing out-of-date equipment or software with new ones. Once you list what standards need to be met to complete your certification, you can create a road map.

4. Design a realistic budget and road map.

Sitting at your conference table with your RP/RPO and department heads is the best way to do this because the standards will affect every employee and every process. CMMC is not just about firewalls and antivirus programs; it includes physical security practices like monitoring guest activity too, so training employees across departments might be necessary.

To create the road map, you'll want to consider things like:

a) Top priority items: which standards don't you meet that put you at the most significant risk? Add those to the beginning of your road map or top of your "to do" list.

b) How much it costs to implement the new or updated standards.

c) Deadlines you must put in place to meet your priority standards first. Allocate your budget to those items. Over the following months, assign parts of your budget to the remaining items as you are able, creating deadlines for each.

I usually tell my clients they should aim to do one new standard every few days to a couple of weeks. It depends on the size of your company. A company of 100 or fewer employees can probably implement some basic controls in a few days. Companies of 10,000 or more may need several weeks. Faster doesn't mean better; it's about taking steps to cross the gap. After this, you'll need to have an auditor come and verify your controls. An RP/RPO can help you schedule that.

DON'T FEAR AUDITORS

Most companies are either Level 1 or Level 2 contractors or subcontractors of DoD programs. I recommend that my clients get CMMC Level 2 certified because this involves a third-party auditor. This is where clients get a bit nervous (auditors can be scary). Don't be scared. Having an auditor assess the state of your cybersecurity hygiene ensures that you know exactly what you need to be compliant, so you're never denied by insurance companies or rejected by prospective clients.

Think of CMMC Level 2 like this. If your car is having issues, you take it to a mechanic. Your mechanic says the brake line needs to be replaced, and it's going to cost you $1,500. You don't know much about cars, but you know you need brakes to stop safely. That's pretty important. Still, $1,500 is a bit of money. Maybe they could patch up the line instead? You decide to bring in a third-party car expert to look at your car. They look at the whole of your car and say, "Hey, your tires are great, your engine looks good, but you need a new brake line." Now you have two people who say you need to replace the brake line to drive your car safely. The alternative is to keep driving your vehicle until your brakes fail, you crash and then you must replace the whole car (and pay some nasty insurance premiums). It's your choice, but to be safe on the road, experts say you need to replace the brake line, but everything else is verified and looks good.

That's what a CMMC auditor does. After your initial assessment, the auditor verifies all the standards. They make sure you have everything you need to operate securely and tell you what you need to become compliant, thus protecting your business, your employees and customer information.

CMMC IS YOUR BRIDGE TO SUCCESS AND SECURITY

Getting from where you are now to being completely CMMC compliant feels like a canyon. I know. It feels like you need binoculars to see across the gap to the other side. Though CMMC feels like the canyon, it's not. Negligent behaviors, inefficient cybersecurity processes and cybercriminals who want to steal confidential company data are the void. CMMC compliance is the bridge. It's the process of creating a flexible infrastructure that will allow you to nimbly adapt to changes in the security industry and keep your business – and future – safe.

Like myself, IT professionals and RP/RPOs are here to make building the bridge feel less daunting. So, grab a cup of coffee and get your team together to discuss what level is right for you. Take it one step at a time and spread your budget out over several months or a year. If you get stuck or have any questions about the process, give me a call.

About Greg

Greg Zimmerle is a Microsoft Certified Systems Engineer, a CMMC Registered Practitioner, and founder and CEO of myIT.com. He knows that running a successful business is about developing processes, aligning yourself with the right people, and delegating effectively.

Running a company is difficult. By the time he was 16 years old, Greg owned and managed a lawn care business with two crews. While in college, he continued this business until one of his clients asked him to take a call from her friend, who was having computer problems. Over the phone, he fixed her friend's issue, and his lawn care client said, "If you know how to fix computers, why are you mowing lawns?" Shortly after this memorable conversation, Greg sold his business. He began building his own computer support company while gaining experience as an IT consultant for Electronic Data Systems in Plano, TX, and working with banks across the country, including Regions Bank, City National Bank and Bank of Houston.

After a few years of building up his expertise and client relationships, he was ready to focus his consulting services on small and medium-sized businesses in his home community in greater Dallas/Fort Worth. During his 25 years as CEO of myIT.com, Greg has served hundreds of wonderful clients who he is proud to call friends.

Greg understands that business owners have a lot on their plates – sales, product delivery, customer service, marketing, accounting, legal, insurance, employees, policies, processes, technology and now compliance, all take up space on a business owner's desk. When Greg saw compliance and regulatory bodies moving into the SMB security landscape, he knew he needed to help his clients prepare. As a CMMC Registered Practitioner, Greg and his team at myIT.com are ready to help clients address the regulations that are in motion now.

The biggest challenge of owning a business, he says, is maintaining the drive it takes to be continuously competitive and successful in an ever-changing business environment. In many ways, the industry's incredible pace is a great benefit to businesses and, in other ways, a challenge. His goal is to reduce the overwhelm while keeping essential security priorities laser focused. He helps clients navigate the strategic direction of their IT, cybersecurity and CMMC compliance complexities by establishing a rhythm for achieving positive results. Cybersecurity is a journey that will never end. The first step, he tells clients, is to figure out where they are now and where they need to be in the next few years. As a cybersecurity security expert, he can help them fill in the gaps.

Greg, his wife, Brenda, and their two dogs, Nikki, and Charlie, enjoy traveling, going to the local lakes, and creating new memories together. Greg plays basketball twice a week, but most of all he loves being a father to his two children, Thomas, and Sarah.

For more information, contact myIT.com:
- Email: greg@myIT.com
- Web: https://www.myit.com

CHAPTER 5

THE SECRET TO MITIGATING YOUR RISK

BY JOE THIGPEN,
Founder & CEO – Datagroup Technologies, Inc.

We are in the middle of a worldwide cyberwar, and you're involved whether or not you like it.

Cyberwarfare isn't like a normal war between countries on land or sea. This war is fought on the Internet, on your computer, your tablet, your cell phone, and your other technology devices. Everyone is a target, and anyone can be a casualty. Trust me, no matter how small your business is, you're a target.

If your security strategy is substandard, all it takes is one bot to find an opening and – boom – you are compromised. Thieves and ransomware gangs love to find the low-hanging fruit of a poorly defended network and take away your access to the data you need to run your business.

Working with the Department of Defense means you may have access to information that America's enemies want to steal or destroy. Therefore, the DoD created the DFARS/CMMC standards (based on NIST standards) to reduce the threats to your business and to government data by applying best-practice security procedures. If you work with the government at all, you most likely need to meet some level of CMMC compliance.

If you've never worked with a cyber-defense company, you may not realize or appreciate the true risks to your business. They are real and there are many. Thankfully, companies like yours don't have to be defenseless. There is a secret to mitigating your risk.

THE REAL RISKS OF POOR CYBERSECURITY

According to Verizon.com, some 60% of small businesses that suffer a cyber-attack go out of business within six months.

That's a scary statistic.

In 2017, Equifax had to settle with the Federal Trade Commission, the Consumer Financial Protection Bureau and all US states and territories to the tune of $575 million (and rising) because they failed to fix a vulnerability and failed to inform the public.

In the same year, Target had to pay an $18.5 million settlement over a breach in 2013, where hackers stole around 40 million credit and debit card accounts during Black Friday, along with the contact information for up to 70 million people. The costs of fixing the breach have reached over $200 million.

One survey[1] of 300 SMBs in the defense industry found that 48% of them had 'severe vulnerabilities' and 10% had critical vulnerabilities and evidence of infiltration. A staggering 28% could not even pass the most basic tier of CMMC requirements.

A smart enemy knows to attack their opponent at the weakest point. Is your company that weakest point in the Defense Industrial Base (DIB) contractor chain? R&D and manufacturing companies are at the greatest risk as of this writing.

---

1. https://www.cpomagazine.com/cyber-security/us-defense-contractors-failing-to-meet-cmmc-requirements-48-have-severe-vulnerabilities/

You may know the basic risks to your company, but it's the second- and third-order risks that shutter businesses. Things like:

a) A loss of revenue during the extended recovery shutdown period. Cyber insurance companies may require forensic audits before allowing the recovery to start.

b) A loss of money spent to recover – if recovery is possible.

c) Loss of money to formally notify everyone involved in the breach, including customers and clients. This cost can be more significant than the recovery.

d) A loss of reputation in the community and industry, leading to fewer contracts and referrals.

e) A loss of existing clients and associated revenue, and vendors who can't trust you now that you've had a security breach.

f) An increase in business and cybersecurity insurance premiums due to proven negligence.

g) A loss of accounts-receivable records, making it unclear who owes you money.

h) A strong possibility of litigation from clients and government agencies.

i) Loss of partnerships and/or subcontractors due to reduced trust.

j) An increase in business and cybersecurity insurance premiums due to a demonstrated high risk.

There are two special risks worth pointing out for DIB contractors:

First, if the government catches wind that a hacker breached your company, you face the loss of government contracts. You could lose your DFARS and CMMC certifications, which could kill your current contracts and prevent you from applying for future ones until you can prove your infrastructure is compliant. You can even be blacklisted from future government contracts.

The second is that the law could hold you personally liable for a cyber-attack. No, being in a corporation will not protect you! The law is coming for stakeholders and board members who hide behind corporate law to protect themselves from cybersecurity liability. You could be sued in civil court for neglecting to implement the standard cybersecurity measures established by NIST and/or the DoD.

ASSESS, IDENTIFY, MITIGATE

The only way to assess, identify and mitigate your security risks for CMMC compliance is to get a comprehensive NIST-based cybersecurity risk assessment conducted by qualified cybersecurity professionals. This is best done through hiring a managed security services provider (MSSP) with a security operations center team. By having access to a SOC, you have someone continuously monitoring and detecting when changes in your network create new vulnerabilities.

Just as you would consult a lawyer to protect you from legal risks, you need a cybersecurity professional to protect you from cyber-attacks. A good cybersecurity company will regularly assess the vulnerabilities of your current system, identify, and explain what those vulnerabilities are, and provide you and your IT team with a strategy to mitigate those vulnerabilities.

Even if you already have cybersecurity staff on your team, an outside pair of eyes is vital to double-check what is happening. It's also an important part of enforcing changes after you're certified. Never think that CMMC, or cybersecurity, is a one-and-done operation!

THE INTERNAL THREAT

Cybersecurity is more than a technical problem. It's a human problem. So many of the requirements are about policies, procedures, documentation, and enforcement. You can have the best technical security and still have it fail because of the human element. In many companies, management policies and a loose cybersecurity culture prevent internal IT staff from implementing cybersecurity to a level that satisfies CMMC requirements.

Third-party companies like an MSSP have the power to push back against dangerous requests from employees and business leaders without facing the threat of losing their jobs or promotion opportunities. Whoever you hire to manage your cybersecurity threat must have the authority to implement and enforce the NIST requirements even above and beyond the whims of the highest leaders of the company.

THE COSTS OF COMPLIANCE

Besides the costs of hiring an MSSP, implementing their recommendations may be more complicated than you think. It may require significant investment in software and hardware upgrades. Let's take an example of using multifactor authentication, or MFA.

Multifactor authentication uses two pieces of information to authenticate a user. One is a password and the other is a random set of numbers updated regularly on a separate device. Just adding this can reduce the risk of account-based compromises by 99%. MFA itself does not cost very much to acquire, and in some cases it's already built into the software you use.

However, your business systems may not currently support MFA technology. Many companies, especially in manufacturing, have legacy systems that have worked for years, or even decades. No one wants to touch them for fear of breaking production. The longer you wait, the easier it will be for a hacker to do the touching.

Yet security upgrades must be done – and are worth the costs. Compare the costs of some downtime and paying for software rewrites to the costs of losing the entire company after a cyber-attack. Compare that cost to losing all future government contracts. As much as it may pain shareholders to bite the bullet, the risks are too great to ignore.

WHAT NEEDS TO BE DONE?

All organizations are subject to, and vulnerable to, threats. These threats may come from seasoned criminals or careless employees. They may cause minor inconveniences, extended service disruptions, severe financial penalties, loss of public trust and damage to corporate reputation.

Identifying an organization's risks is the first step toward protecting the confidentiality, integrity, and availability of critical information assets. It is also an important component of achieving regulatory, commercial, and organizational compliance.

These risks must be prioritized based on the organization's vulnerabilities, the motivation of existing threat sources, the costs of remediation, the probability that existing vulnerabilities will be exploited and other factors.

CMMC compliance is really about complying with NIST guidelines. The National Institute of Standards and Technology created these guidelines as the current gold standard for cybersecurity frameworks. If you follow these guidelines and can prove you followed these standards, you'll be on solid footing for defending yourself.

Below, I summarize the guidelines required by CMMC 2.0 to comply with the three levels:

1. Level 1 – 17 specific guidelines found in NIST SP 800-171
2. Level 2 – All remaining guidelines in NIST SP 800-171
3. Level 3 – All of NIST SP 800-171 along with NIST
   SP 800-172

The first best step is to get your company at least to CMMC 2.0 Level 1 compliance. Even though it's only 17 items, they cover a lot of ground. However, if you're handling Controlled Unclassified Information, then you must go for Level 2 certification, with 110 control requirements and assessment done at least once every three years, with regular reporting during the period based on your contract severity.

The secret to mitigating risk is now clear. You need outside help that knows these guidelines inside and out and has the authority to assess your company's vulnerabilities, mitigate them and secure them from attacks both inside and outside your company.

CMMC assessments are now part of the cost of doing business with the DoD.

STEPS TO TAKE RIGHT NOW TO PROTECT YOUR SYSTEMS

If you don't have an MSSP or a cybersecurity professional on your staff, here are some basic first steps to take right now to mitigate your risk.

Step 1: Create and Test Backups Now

There is absolutely no security software on the market that can guarantee 100% protection from threats, including data loss. The only sure protection against data loss is an excellent backup strategy. You must create multiple backups per day on-site and off-site at a secure location. If your strategy does not implement multiple copies in multiple locations, it's not good enough!

Ransomware, currently the biggest payload for attacks, encrypts the drives in a system, and the hacker then demands payment to decrypt it. Payment won't always get your data back, plus it shows that you're willing to negotiate, and you become a constant target afterward.

Test your backups to ensure you can recover from them if needed. There are many horror stories in IT of backups that failed when they were needed most because they weren't tested!

Step 2: Patch Your Systems

One technique that hackers use is to set a scanner to look for a particular vulnerability, then try it on any address they can find. It's much like a car thief going through a parking lot and trying doors, or a burglar using a bump key to bypass your dead bolt.

IT manufacturers constantly release patches to fix these vulnerabilities, but it is up to you to apply them. This is a fundamental cybersecurity practice that is overlooked in many organizations.

If you are breached and the forensics show you failed to apply a security patch that could have prevented it, you could be held liable, lose your government contracts and much more. Cyber insurance companies can also decline payouts and further coverage when negligence is proven.

Step 3: Get Your Professional Security Assessment Completed

You may already have great cybersecurity knowledge and practices at your company. You might even comply with Level 1 already. Yet even the largest DIB companies with their own SOCs can use the help of an outside MSSP to help with their security, and they'll need one anyway once the DoD requires regular third-party assessments.

One of my favorite sayings is, "We don't know what we don't know." This is never truer than when speaking about network security. A cybersecurity compliance assessment will present you and your stakeholders with the good, the bad and the ugly of your network, and it will tell you exactly what items must be addressed to be secure and compliant.

Once you or your chosen MSSP has mitigated all the issues, you will be able to satisfactorily submit your CMMC scores to meet your compliance deadlines. You will also sleep much better at night, knowing you are the reason your business is so much safer.

Step 4: Continuously Educate Everyone about Cybersecurity

It's critical to know that cyberwarfare is always ongoing. New attacks and vulnerabilities get discovered all the time. If you do your due diligence, especially with the help of an outside MSSP who can watch your network 24/7, the odds of a successful breach will drop dramatically.

When your employees know about how cyber-attackers operate, they can take steps to defend themselves. They should know about things like ransomware, phishing attacks, the dangers of bringing in unsecured devices like USB drives and the risks associated with breaches.

Make it personal. Tell them how a breach of the network could make them lose their job and get the company to lose CMMC compliance. Make them understand that this could destroy the business, and that they have a responsibility to know how to defend themselves when they're targeted by a cyber-attack.

Step 5: Trust but Verify

Cybersecurity cannot be put on autopilot. It must be managed daily by qualified security professionals and maintained daily. Then, to close the loop and monitor risk to the organization, we must require regular reporting from these professionals, so we know the risks are being adequately controlled. In other words, "Trust but verify."

WHAT'S THE SECRET?

The secret to mitigating risk is now clear. Cybersecurity is serious business. Whether you require CMMC compliance or not, you need cybersecurity professionals to advise and/or mitigate your risk of compromise and to keep a watchful eye on your security around the clock.

Someone who knows the guidelines inside and out, like an MSSP familiar with CMMC compliance, can help you assess the risk, mitigate the risk, and build a formidable cybersecurity strategy to protect your business, your employees, your clients, your reputation, and everything that is important to you. If you are required to be DFARS/CMMC compliant, select a security company that is certified to advise you.

Should you have any questions about what to do next, don't hesitate to contact me.

Stay safe.

About Joe

Joe Thigpen is the founder and CEO of Datagroup Technologies, Inc. (DTI), a managed IT security and IT services provider based out of Eastern North Carolina. His company manages and supports businesses and government organizations across the country 24/7.

Joe is no stranger to defending assets and mitigating risk. He spent his first 20 years in the US Army as a paratrooper in the 82nd Airborne Division and Long-Range Reconnaissance. As an army combat veteran, Joe understands what it means to defend against enemy attacks. This fuels his passion for cyberdefense.

After returning to civilian life and finishing an IT degree in 2001, he saw that the standard of security and IT services in his area was poor and realized that most computer service companies and repair shops lacked the experience and knowledge necessary to adequately support and defend business networks. He set out to build one of the area's first professional network management firms, now referred to as managed services providers (MSPs).

For the last 20 years, he and his company of 20+ engineers and cybersecurity professionals have secured networks and provided managed IT services for small businesses all the way to the enterprise level. Over the years, as cyberthreats evolved, Joe has stayed ahead of the curve by constantly upgrading his cybersecurity arsenal.

Today, DTI is also considered a managed security services provider (MSSP) by operating its own Compliance and Security Operations Center. DTI's SOC is manned with cybersecurity professionals 24 hours a day to detect, identify and respond to cybersecurity threats against the networks that he and his security teams protect more quickly. Staying ahead of the curve and putting security first are why Joe's clients have remained safe and operational for 20+ years.

Thanks to Joe's decades of military and IT experience, he is one of the most uniquely qualified people to understand the threats of today's cyberwar, and how to explain to business owners what they need to do to avoid becoming a casualty in this new style of warfare and prevent data from entering the wrong hands.

For more information, contact Joe:
- Email: jthigpen@dtinetworks.com
- Web: https://dtinetworks.com/ or https://www.linkedin.com/in/joe-thigpen
-22428814/

CHAPTER 6

WHAT IS YOUR CYBER-HYGIENE SCORE?

FIND OUT IF YOU'RE DOING GREAT OR ARE IN DANGER, AND WHERE TO START

BY DAVID LUFT,
CEO – LDD Consulting

Becoming a United States Government contractor is a lucrative proposition, but it also comes with a great deal more red tape than working in the private sector. If you want to win contracts with the Department of Defense, then the complexity climbs higher, as it should. Could you imagine handling DoD information without requirements on how to protect it? Even if you aren't working directly with the DoD, but you're a subcontractor or anywhere in the supply chain, you too are required to be Cybersecurity Maturity Model Certification (CMMC) compliant.

While a cyber-hygiene score sounds like something your dentist made up to get you to brush more, it's a vital and honest assessment of your company's readiness to handle cyberthreats and can measure how you stand up to CMMC compliance. It's about following procedures and steps to keep your network and information safe. Much like your personal hygiene, it's based on discipline and consistency. If you make it part of your everyday life, it will become mechanical, and you won't have to wonder where you stand – it will just be a part of your routine.

CORE CYBER-HYGIENE STRATEGIES

So, you've decided to go after those DoD contracts, and you want to know where you stand. Let's get started by reviewing what I call core cyber-hygiene strategies and then we'll dive deeper into them. These are the things that need to be put in place to ensure a reputable cyber-hygiene score. They include:

- Core Security and Access Controls (including firewalls, antivirus, and backups)
- Employee Training and Personnel Security
- Monitoring, Maintenance and Configuration Management
- Policies and Procedures
- Security Assessments, Auditing, and Accountability
- Incident Response
- Risk Management (including subcontractors)

CORE SECURITY AND ACCESS CONTROL

Core security and access controls are big categories. They encompass your systems and network security, but also physical security and access to your facilities. I know some of your eyes just glazed over a bit, but stick with me because this stuff is important, and I'll try to address it with the assumption that you have little-to-zero knowledge of networking and technology.

First, let's talk about authentication and authorization. Authentication means verifying that you are who you say you are. We accomplish this with individual network credentials with secure passwords that prove you are the person you claim to be. Authorization means accepting your credentials from authentication, but then determining what you can do. To break these down to non-technical examples, we'll look at it in the context of physical security. When you start a new job and you get a badge with your picture on it, that allows people to see that your face matches your badge, so that's authentication and identity. Later that day, you're roaming the building and you see a door with a badge reader on it. You decide to look inside, but you're not allowed to enter that room – when your badge is scanned, you are denied entry. That is authorization.

Firewalls are a lot like locks on doors but apply to your network and computers. Firewall rules determine WHO can get to WHAT resources on your network. They can be physical pieces of equipment or, if you're a small operation, they may just be software that's embedded in your router, which is what connects you to the Internet. Firewalls work with allow-and-deny rules. Older firewalls used Internet protocol addresses as the WHO, but many of the modern options can even allow/deny based on your network credentials. The WHAT refers to other computers or equipment on the network. If you have a server with data that shouldn't be accessible by everyone, then by default you deny all traffic to it, then put in rules that allow only specific persons or computers to get to that machine.

Another important part of this category is virus and malware detection and prevention. Ninety-five percent of cybersecurity breaches are a result of human error. This is often because someone clicks a link in an email they shouldn't or opens a document from email or a website they don't recognize. While antivirus and zero trust software can't stop all incidents, they will prevent many of them. Although it's not enough just to have these features, you should keep them updated with the latest virus definitions, because the bad guys are constantly finding new ways to exploit your systems.[1]

Now that your network has firewalls, you know the identity of the people on your network and you have up-to-date antivirus

---

1. Cybint (December 23, 2020), "15 Alarming Cyber Security Facts and Stats." https://www.cybintsolutions.com/cyber-security-facts-stats/

software installed, you need to make sure you have backups, and you can restore them. Ideally, you back up every computer and device on your network, but you must, at a minimum, have regular backups of your important systems. Imagine the fallout when you've been working on a major project for weeks and your system suffers a catastrophic failure. This could be your laptop or a database on one of your servers. Either way, it's going to be a terrible day, but your day will get much worse if you don't have backups of the critical data.

Your backups should be automated – not something you even have to think about daily. You should also have offline backups of your backup files. What does that mean? If your backups run to disk, you need to back up those backup files somewhere that can't be reached as easily. This can be to the cloud or external devices you unplug when not actively backing up. The reason: ransomware attacks don't only try to encrypt the files on your machines, they also try to find and encrypt your backup files. So, if you don't take the extra step, you won't be able to recover the backups to get your business up and running again. Restores are the other part of the equation – backups are useless if you can't restore them. You should test restoring your backups on a regular basis to avoid surprises. If a hacker wipes out important data and you can't restore it, your best option will be to update your résumé, because then it's too late.

EMPLOYEE TRAINING AND PERSONNEL SECURITY

Earlier we talked about antivirus software and how most cybersecurity breaches are the result of human error. The antivirus software can only do so much, as hackers are finding new ways to breach every day, and the software makers can't always keep up. All employees in your company need to have comprehensive cybersecurity training, regardless of their role. The importance of this training needs to rank as high as the human resource training we all take when starting a new job, and it also needs to be reinforced with ongoing training to keep the concepts fresh in the minds of your employees and keep them abreast of new scams and attack types to be aware of.

Personnel security doesn't refer to having security to escort people to their cars at night, but to vetting employees based on conduct and character for positions with the government. This includes doing proper pre-employment screenings and terminating employees who violate conduct policies or show moral or ethical failings. It seeks to minimize risks posed by workers to the organization's assets.[2]

Personnel Security:
The discipline of assessing the conduct, integrity, judgment, loyalty, reliability, and stability of individuals for duties and responsibilities requiring trustworthiness.[3]

MONITORING, MAINTENANCE AND CONFIGURATION MANAGEMENT

You've implemented some processes we've outlined, and now you need to monitor and maintain them. How will you know if something has changed or that you have operating systems or applications running outdated versions and what will you do to fix them? You need to monitor your systems and your physical space. CMMC Level 1 requires escorting visitors and monitoring their activity, as well as managing physical devices like USB keys. For systems monitoring, you need to monitor your network and boundary systems. Implementing an intrusion detection system to alert you of network irregularities is also a good idea.

For maintenance, you can't dismiss this or "kick the can" further down the road. Outdated applications and operating systems don't get patches or upgrades released as often and are perfect targets

---

2. National Institute of Standards and Technology (June 2017), "An Introduction to Information Security." https://nvlpubs.nist.gov/nistpubs/SpecialPublications/NIST.SP.800-12r1.pdf
   3. Computer Security Resource Center, Glossary. https://csrc.nist.gov/glossary/term/personnel_security

for hackers looking to exploit vulnerabilities. You also must have regular patching schedules to apply any security patches released by vendors. A security patch can be released because of a known issue that's already in the wild, but it could also be one that hasn't yet been discovered by hackers. If it's the latter, then hackers are learning about it when the patch gets released and they'll start working to exploit it, so the sooner you apply it, the better.

Configuration management refers to storing and knowing the state of your systems. There are many software packages out there that can help with this, but its job is to look for changes to a system, and it can even be told to restore it anytime it finds a deviation. The basic principle here is that you need to know what your system is supposed to look like, know when it's changed and who changed it.

POLICIES AND PROCEDURES

Your employees can't follow policies and procedures that aren't known and documented. Even less strict frameworks, like HIPAA and Sarbanes–Oxley, require you to have these documented, so you know it's going to be necessary if you work for the government. I won't dive into everything that should be included in those policies and procedures, but you must have them, and everyone in your company should know their location and contents. It's even a good idea to request that employees read and acknowledge them every year.

SECURITY ASSESSMENTS AND AUDITS

The security assessments are a bedrock of CMMC compliance. Most businesses will outsource these assessments to a company like LDD Consulting, which specializes in this type of work. The time invested and level of effort to perform these tasks internally will be exponentially harder for the uninitiated. The results of the assessments tell the government if you can maintain your compliance. If you choose to self-assess, which will be allowed for some companies in CMMC 2.0, make sure you report accurately and honestly, or you could in violation of the False Claims Act.

> *The False Claims Act (FCA), 31 U.S.C. §§ 3729–3733 was enacted in 1863 by a Congress concerned that suppliers of goods to the Union Army during the Civil War were defrauding the Army. The FCA provided that any person who knowingly submitted false claims to the government was liable for double the government's damages plus a penalty of $2,000 for each false claim.*[4]

Auditing has many contexts in the business world and even within the context of this book. You need to have auditing turned on for your systems, you need to audit your security controls regularly and you should even hire third-party companies to perform audits. Just as public companies are required to have financial audits, you need to have someone perform security audits. This may include hiring someone to do penetration testing, where someone tries to gain access to your systems with brute force or through known vulnerabilities. Some companies hire people to try social engineering campaigns to see if your employees will unwittingly give up private information that can game your security controls. Hiring ethical hackers to find soft spots in your company to gain entry is another example. One other part of auditing is that you should collect the logs from all your systems into a central location. This makes it easier to analyze them and makes it more difficult for hackers to clean up after themselves if they breach one of your systems.

INCIDENT RESPONSE

What happens if your business is hacked? Let's face it, in today's climate it's more like WHEN you're hacked. You need to have a response plan. Whether this is an internal process or through a partner, it's essential to know what you're going to do BEFORE

---

4. The United States Department of Justice, "The False Claims Act: A Primer." https://www.justice.gov/sites/default/files/civil/legacy/2011/04/22/ C-FRAUDS_FCA_Primer.pdf

the breach occurs. If you're the victim of a ransomware attack, for example, and you don't have your incident response planned out, it could take weeks or even months before you're back to business as usual. That can cost your company a lot of money and likely damage your reputation. Sure, your reputation may take a minor hit just for being hacked, but it happens so frequently today that how you recover will be what gets the most attention. If you're back up and running in a day or two, it will show your resiliency.

RISK MANAGEMENT

For information system security, risk management means limiting the risk to an organization's operations and assets. As it applies to CMMC, any project handling Controlled Unclassified Information is expected to have a defined risk management approach. While the CMMC is not overly prescriptive in its details on what the approach should include, it's the culmination of all the items included in my core cyber-hygiene strategies we've been walking through. The buck doesn't stop with you though – if you are the prime contractor, this also applies to subcontractors in the supply chain. It is your responsibility to ensure your subcontractors also meet the requirements.

CONCLUSION

The road to a good cyber-hygiene score is difficult, but it's necessary for gaining CMMC compliance and scaling the mountain that is DoD contracting. The government needs private-sector contractors to unearth new ideas and innovate the next generation of concepts and designs to keep our country safe and keep us on the leading edge of technological advancements.

Keep in mind that the government knows this process is arduous and the price of admission is steep, and the contracts awarded allow for that burden. There are a lot of companies these days that offer their services to perform the assessments. At LDD Consulting, we take a different approach, as we know that getting those results is just the beginning. As a company rooted in managed services, we don't just drop the assessment on your desk and move on to the next project. If you want our help with implementation, maintenance and the ongoing work needed to stay current, we'll roll up our sleeves and get our hands dirty. If you already have a trusted implementation contractor or team, that's fine as well. We strive to offer the best service and customer service, so we're here for any of your business needs.

About David

David Luft is the CEO of LDD Consulting. He founded the company in 2002 with Dina, his wife since 1992. LDD Consulting is a Managed Services Provider of IT services. The original focus of the company was on education and medical businesses because they're in environments that require compliance, security and automation and often don't have the internal resources to manage them. With the daily increase in cyberthreats, LDD Consulting has added cybersecurity and government compliance to its arsenal of offerings.

When David was in high school, his father told him he had to take a foreign language, so he signed up for Spanish. That didn't go so well, and he failed. His father still required him to take a foreign language and suggested computer programming, which in the early '80s was still very much foreign. After that, David was all in and never wanted to do anything else.

David was a Microsoft Certified Trainer and previously taught the Microsoft Certified Systems Engineer certification at the University of Phoenix, ITT Tech, and the University of New Mexico. He started working toward a Bachelor of Computer Science, but upon taking some psychology classes needed for his studies in artificial intelligence, he found he enjoyed the subject and finished with a Bachelor's in Psychology with a minor in Computer Science. He later completed his MBA with a focus on Information Technology.

David and Dina have two grown children they're extremely proud of, a son and a daughter. David credits Dina's positivity for their children growing up to be caring and giving people. They also have three grandchildren who they adore. When David isn't protecting companies from cyberthreats, he can often be found hiking or backpacking in the New Mexico high desert. He and Dina also love camping with their expanding family and get out on a boat any time the opportunity presents itself.

Contact LDD Consulting:
- Email: info@lddconsulting.com
- Web: https://lddconsulting.com/
- Phone: 505-792-2375

CHAPTER 7

WHY THESE NINE CMMC BEST PRACTICES ARE CRITICAL FOR SMBS

BY AUSTIN JUSTICE,
VP & Owner – Justice IT Computing

Most small businesses aren't prepared for a cyber-attack. In fact, only 5% of small business owners consider cybersecurity the biggest risk to their business.[1] Here's another fact. Sixty-seven percent of the businesses awarded Department of Defense contracts are small businesses.[2] In total, there are approximately 300,000 organizations, including large enterprises and small businesses, that make up the DoD supply chain, either as prime contractors, subcontractors or vendors and suppliers – all contributing in some way to our national security.

Malicious cyber activities are increasing. Bad state and non-state actors are working overtime to undermine US security. The federal government has committed to standardizing cybersecurity practices across the defense industrial base, in all aspects of acquisition programs, extending to all members of the acquisition workforce. Now, more than ever, small businesses can no longer ignore the very real implications of inadequate cybersecurity – especially if they want to continue to work with the government.

That's why the DoD has developed the Cybersecurity Maturity Model Certification, known as CMMC.[3]

CMMC is a framework of cybersecurity standards that mirrors the US Government's NIST SP 800-171 and 172, special publications first implemented on June 18, 2015, that provide recommended requirements for safeguarding the confidentiality of Federal Contract Information (FCI) and Controlled Unclassified Information (CUI). But since CMMC's first iteration, the DoD has struggled with low compliance rates. CMMC aims to solve that problem.

In early 2019, the DoD began developing the CMMC framework in response to increased cybersecurity attacks and data-theft incidents involving the unlawful acquisition of significant amounts of sensitive defense information from defense industrial base systems. Put simply, CMMC sets the minimum cybersecurity requirements for companies doing business with the government.

Currently on its second iteration, CMMC now has three security tiers:

1. Foundational (Level 1)
2. Advanced (Level 2)
3. Expert (Level 3)

Level 1 applies only to contractors who focus on the protection of FCI data. Level 2 applies to contractors working with CUI data. And Level 3 applies to contractors working with CUI data on the DoD's highest priority programs and is focused on reducing the risk of advanced persistent threats. Fortunately, most businesses will require a Level 1 or Level 2 certification.

The tier that a contractor needs to comply with is based on the types of data they work with to execute federal contracts. Both CUI and FCI include information created or collected by or for the government, as well as information received from the government.

FCI is any information that is not intended for public release and is subject to minimum cybersecurity requirements, including, but not limited to:

- emails originating from government addresses
- systems that store files received from the government
- hard storage devices
- workstations
- manufacturing devices
- backup systems
- networks

CUI is data that requires safeguarding and may also be subject to dissemination controls. Although it isn't considered classified, legally, it cannot be released to the public and must be protected in the interest of national security. Examples of CUI include, but are not limited to:

- legal material
- health documents
- technical drawings and blueprints
- intellectual property

WHO NEEDS CMMC CERTIFICATION?

Think of CMMC as the golden ticket for businesses that want to work with the government, whether directly or indirectly. Without it, you can't bid on, win, or participate in a contract.

Let's look at the DoD contract puzzle.

For instance, Lockheed Martin is the world's largest defense contractor by revenue, and last year it received $72.9 billion in funds paid out by the Pentagon.[4] They serve as the prime contractor for the F-35 Lightning II fighter jet – the most modern fighter jet in the world. But they couldn't do it without a global supply chain of more than 1,900 companies based in the US and in every nation acquiring the F-35. From metal fabricators to electrical harness manufacturers to producers of magnetic technologies to labor staffing – everybody who "touches" the F-35 is part of the DoD supply chain and subject to CMMC certification. By incorporating cybersecurity standards into acquisition programs, CMMC provides the DoD assurance that contractors and subcontractors are meeting its cybersecurity requirements.

The path to CMMC certification is filled with complexities and nuances. To help you prepare for and navigate your own CMMC journey, here are nine best practices I've compiled while working with my own clients on their way to compliance:

#1. DETERMINE YOUR "WHY"

The US engages in cyberwar every day against threats to the industrial base, national security and our partners and allies. In 2021, government and military sectors saw a 47% increase in cyber-attack attempts.[5] They realized they needed standards in place to address digital security issues like state-sponsored cyber-attacks and inadequate cybersecurity measures by subcontractors. That's the DoD's "why" for asking for CMMC certification. Now, what's your "why" for complying?

You aren't a Lockheed Martin or Boeing of the DoD supply chain, but maybe you are supplying a small plastic piece or a larger forged component to one of the big guys. Or maybe you are a consultant or a staffing specialist for a larger defense contractor. If you can check any of these boxes, then you are considered part of the DoD supply chain and therefore subject to CMMC certification. Maybe the product or service you are supplying to the contractor isn't your bread and butter, but it's still a decent portion of your revenue that you don't want to give up. The first step in the compliance process begins with understanding why you need to be compliant.

But there's another reason to go down the CMMC path. Small and medium businesses are easier targets for hackers because they often lack resources and security expertise. This is an opportunity for you to increase your own cybersecurity measures. After all, if the government is going to make you protect their data, shouldn't you want to protect yours and that of your other clients as well? Safeguarding data is the ultimate purpose of CMMC – use it to your advantage.

#2.   MANAGE YOUR CYBERSECURITY EXPECTATIONS

Cyber-attacks are more sophisticated and coming faster than ever, making it nearly impossible to eliminate every threat. When you build a system of compliance and policies around that inevitability, you'll be better prepared to respond, isolate, and communicate an incident. CMMC compliance isn't something you can set to autopilot, walk away, and check a box that says you're compliant. Everything about it requires management, maintenance and putting the work in every day.

#3.   UNDERSTAND THE CONCEPT OF LEAST PRIVILEGE

The principle of least privilege requires that you restrict user accounts, devices, or services to only the permissions that users and programs need to perform their work. This is a requirement of the CMMC certification. Limiting the privileges an account has limits the security risks associated with that account. The goal behind the principle of least privilege is to ensure that only a few individuals have administrative privileges on an information system to prevent accidental and intentional harm. But the use of an administrator account should be used only when necessary.

As an IT administrator, owner, or manager for your business, you should not be using a privileged account to perform day-to-day work like sending and receiving emails. You need to get in the habit of logging in and out of your admin account when going between non-privileged and privileged functions. If you are troubleshooting a device or setting up new user accounts, that's when you use the admin – or privileged – account.

#4. LEVERAGE TECHNOLOGY TO MAKE CMMC COMPLIANCE EASIER

CMMC compliance requires some extensive documentation to prove that your business is doing its part to safeguard your data and systems. For example, under CMMC regulations, you have to review every single security and change log. Manually studying logs requires time, diligence and manpower. But there are AI and automation tools available to make the process easier. They scan your log data and alert you to any risk-level anomalies detected.

#5. TAKE A HOLISTIC APPROACH TO CYBERSECURITY

A lot of businesses make the assumption that if they have cybersecurity, they're compliant, or if they're compliant, they have cybersecurity. There's a bit of a gap in there.

What you should do first is focus on the security, and then address compliance. Ultimately, what you need is to be secure, and then compliance is the piece where you get to prove you are secure.

A compliance-first initiative typically results in business inefficiencies. A process that may have originally taken 40 minutes could turn into two hours of logging and encrypting, just to satisfy the compliance. If you start with security first, there's a way to approach it where you can satisfy the compliance but also keep running as efficiently as possible.

#6. UNDERSTAND WHY YOU HAVE TO STAY ON TOP OF DOCUMENTATION

Essentially, through the lens of CMMC compliance, your documentation is there to prove that you're not negligent. It has to be managed and collected, day after day and year after year. It's not something you can throw together two weeks ahead of an audit. Every change log, every ticket – even every time someone gets locked out of their user account and you have to change the password – you must literally show this in a CMMC audit.

#7. PREPARE FOR THE INEVITABLE BREACH

To prepare for compliance, you have to start with the assumption that a breach or an incident is inevitable. That's why a huge part of CMMC compliance is having a recovery plan in place. The more thorough the plan, the less disruption your company will experience following a security incident.

Detailed policies and procedures should include how you will isolate your assets as soon as the breach occurs, assess the breach, communicate to your affected customers and authorities, and restore your assets.

Remember, your goal is to create a cybersecurity system that's good enough to prevent most attacks. You can lock your systems down to a point where maybe you won't ever get hacked, but then you can't do business.

#8. SELF-CHECK YOUR CURRENT CYBERSECURITY PRACTICES

Before you start your CMMC journey, take a look at your current cybersecurity efforts. Being honest with yourself about what your business is doing today for security is the first best step. Are your cybersecurity tools up-to-date? Are you routinely performing backups? Are all devices

– onsite or remote – password protected? Are devices containing sensitive materials encrypted? Are you using multifactor authentication? Have you fully identified CUI and FCI data, how it's being used, who has access to it? These are just some cybersecurity basics, but the best place to start is ahead of obtaining CMMC compliance.

Additionally, CMMC success is dependent on every single person in your business practicing cybersecurity hygiene every time they touch technology. From your admin assistants to the CEO, if you do business with DoD directly or indirectly, cybersecurity is everyone's responsibility if you want to maintain that business.

#9. OUTSOURCE YOUR CMMC COMPLIANCE

CMMC compliance is not just cybersecurity. With up to 110 security controls required by CMMC, the process can get complicated. That's why you shouldn't go it alone. Even if you have your own internal IT professional, or team, they're busy working on the digital initiatives and internal projects that are moving your business forward. CMMC is just a distraction for them.

We recognize that small and medium-sized businesses just don't have the time or expertise to devote the hundreds of hours required to reach and maintain CMMC certification correctly. We can provide the solution.

CMMC isn't something we dabble in. It's what we specialize in. We've worked with defense contractors and their suppliers on cybersecurity initiatives since 2017. We have a proven turnkey system that's process-driven and intentional. We complete your assessment and provide you with a CMMC Report Card. Together, we develop your System Security Plan and Plan of Action and Milestones (POAM). We then implement the POAM to get you ready for your audit.

Our streamlined security assessment process allows for your assessment to be conducted in a timely manner, so you can continue meeting your contractual requirements.

CONCLUSION

Simple self-attestation, or saying you are CMMC compliant, may likely not be allowed for bidding on new work – particularly if you fall under the CMMC Level 2 category for prioritized acquisitions.

Bottom line, CMMC isn't best adopted as a DIY approach. Your contracts depend on your CMMC compliance being done correctly. The process can be arduous if you aren't experienced, and consume significant resources trying to figure it out. Outsourcing CMMC to a third party with expert capabilities will help ensure a return on your investment and free up your internal IT and cybersecurity team for more impactful projects.

Sources

1. Laura Wronski (May 21, 2022), "America's Small Businesses Aren't Ready for a Cyberattack." https://www.cnbc.com/2022/05/21/americas-small-businesses-arent-ready-for-a-cyberattack.html
2. C. Todd Lopez (November 16, 2020), "Small Businesses Key to Nation's Defense." U.S. Department of Defense News, https://www.defense.gov/News/News-Stories/Article/Article/2416891/small-businesses-key-to-nations-defense/
3. CMMC FAQs. https://www.acq.osd.mil/cmmc/faq.html
4. Jerome Becquart (December 30, 2022), "Ready for CMMC? Here's How You Can Get There." https://federalnewsnetwork.com/commentary/2020/12/ready-for-cmmc-heres-how-you-can-get-there/
5. Summer Myatt (October 22, 2021), "Lockheed Martin Tops Defense Contract Recipients List in New DOD FY 2020 Defense Spending Report." https://executivegov.com/2021/10/lockheed-martin-tops-defense-contract-list-in-new-dod-fy-2020-defense-spending-r/

About Austin

Austin Justice is the Vice President and Owner of Justice IT Consulting. The Burleson, TX–based firm was founded in 2003 to provide technology solutions and cybersecurity services to small and midsize manufacturers in the Dallas–Fort Worth metroplex.

Justice IT Consulting specializes in CMMC and DFARS compliance, assisting Department of Defense contractors and suppliers in meeting the government's cybersecurity requirements.

Austin's expertise in CMMC compliance began in 2017, when he partnered with a lieutenant colonel and commander of the United States Air Forces' 21st Network Warfare Squadron and, later, deputy of the Air Force's Cyber Forward Program to start Cyber Forward, Inc. This is where he helped develop a streamlined security assessment process to aid defense contractors in meeting their contractual compliance requirements in two weeks.

Under Austin's leadership, Justice IT Consulting has gained recognition as a leading cybersecurity service provider to manufacturing businesses throughout DFW and beyond. The firm's turnkey CMMC services are highly sought, offering a variety of strategies, including onsite engineering support, state-of-the-art tools and software, network setup, and writing and implementing the required policy documents on their customers' behalf.

Austin holds a Bachelor of Applied Science degree in Agricultural and Applied Economics from Texas Tech University and several industry certifications, including CompTIA, Panduit and Cisco.

He is the author of IT Scams, the ultimate small-business owner's guide to finding a professional, competent, honest, considerate, on-time, fairly-priced, and dependable computer consultant. Additionally, he has authored two articles on cybersecurity and HIPPA compliance. The first, "Ask The Expert Series: Requirements For HIPAA Compliance: The Key Channel Partner Challenges," is a discussion of Health Insurance Portability and Accountability Act challenges from an IT services provider perspective. The second, "6 Ways To Improve The Security In Your Offering," explains how a managed IT services provider can help small and medium businesses by integrating security into their business offerings.

Austin is active in his community in several long-term and short-term capacities, including serving as a board member of the Chisholm Trail 100 Club, a nonprofit organization that supports the families of injured or fallen first responders in Johnson, Somervell and Hood Counties, as well as the City of Mansfield. Additionally, he served as a member of the Burleson Independent School District Facilities Advisory Committee. Their mission is to engage and support every learner with a rigorous curriculum, so they graduate college and are "Career- Ready."

Contact Information:
- Phone: 817-803-4603
- Email: info@justiceitc.com
- Web: https://www.cmmc-texas.com/
- Address: 740 SW Wilshire Blvd., Suite 100, Burleson, TX 76028
- LinkedIn: https://www.linkedin.com/in/austinjustice

CHAPTER 8

HOW <u>NOT</u> TAKING COMPLIANCE AS A CULTURE SERIOUSLY CAN DESTROY YOUR COMPANY

BY JOHN HILL,
Founder & CEO – TechSage Solutions

"I don't know that much about cyber, but I do think that's the number one problem with mankind."

The statement above was made by billionaire businessman Warren Buffett at the May 6, 2017, shareholder meeting of Berkshire Hathaway. Buffett went on to say that cyber-attacks are a bigger threat to humanity than nuclear weapons. I've spent much of my working life in cybersecurity and compliance. Based on my experiences serving as a communications security analyst in the US Air Force Security Service during the Vietnam War and later being involved in the early stages of cybersecurity, I find it hard to disagree with Buffett.

Fortunately, more and more, Defense Industrial Base businesses are starting to understand that Cybersecurity Maturity Model Certification (CMMC) is not just "more unnecessary government regulations." Company owners and managers realize it is a critical requirement necessary to protect our Department of Defense (DoD) and safeguard our country from cybercriminals. From data theft to cyber-attacks and ransomware attacks, cyberhackers are costing the DoD and its contractors and subcontractors billions of dollars each year and, in the process, making our country much less secure. A case in point is the fifth-generation F-35 Lightning II stealth fighter and its three variants. It's believed that China stole the information about the F-35 from the United States and used it to develop their own advanced fifth-generation stealth fighter, the J-20.

The threat is very real, and it's omnipotent, and if you care about our national security, you should do everything you can to protect it from foreign cybercriminals, which is the intent behind CMMC. But, of course, in addition to protecting our country, it's also about protecting your business and your DoD clients. If you hesitate too long, or neglect to take any action at all, one click of the mouse by one of your employees could destroy everything you've worked so hard to build.

One of the current pitfalls your business could fall prey to is not accurately completing the National Institute of Standards and Technology Special Publication (NIST SP 800-171) self-assessment, submitting your score to the Supplier Performance Risk System (SPRS) and preparing your system security plan and your Plan of Actions and Milestones. Because there's no third party involved to verify that what you are doing is what the government expects, your business may be tempted to adopt a more cavalier attitude than the situation warrants. For example, when CMMC came out, we'd speak to a business about the certification process and they'd say to us, "Well, we don't have to worry about that anymore. We can just say 'yes,' that we do all this stuff, and they're not going to assess us beyond that."

It's a risky and potentially-costly attitude to take. Many businesses do not know how to score themselves properly. Many give themselves a perfect SPRS score of 110. The Defense Contract Management Agency's Defense Industrial Base Cybersecurity Assessment Center (DIBCAC) is doing audits and finding that the high score the businesses give themselves often doesn't represent their reality. One company awarded itself an almost perfect score of 105. When the government audited them, they found their real score was minus 100. According to DoD estimations, 75% of the companies with SPRS scores scored themselves 110 out of 110. Two years of DIBCAC assessments revealed that 75% of those had seriously deficient programs and only 25% qualified as being "mostly implemented."

When we audit a company that has already done a self-assessment, we rarely come up with a score anywhere near their self-assessment SPRS score. It's not because the company is trying to deceive the government. Usually, it's a combination of them being less strict than a third-party assessor would be, and their lack of a true understanding of what many of the questions really mean. For instance, if they don't understand something, instead of doing some research to find out exactly what was expected of them, they just say, "Yes, we do it." A high self-assessment score often triggers the government to take a closer look to see if that score is warranted or not. We've seen that when a business shows a high score, they usually weren't able to achieve it without some outside help.

Once CMMC is ratified and begins showing up as a requirement in your contracts, a high-level executive in your company must attest to the DoD that your company's self-assessment of complying with CMMC Level 1 is accurate and complete. In most cases, the executive isn't the one doing the self-assessment and doesn't know the nuts and bolts of what's required, so they must trust the employees who are completing the self-assessment. If the employee doesn't fully grasp the meaning of each of the questions asked, it could have severe consequences for the executive who signed off on the self-assessment, such as the business being prosecuted under the False Claims Act. My advice to any business that requires CMMC Level 1 is to take it extremely seriously. I strongly recommend that every business, regardless of whether or not they do business with the DoD, should strive for the equivalent of Level 1 compliance.

Besides the additional labor and general hassle of posting an incorrect self-assessment score, here are five ways it can be detrimental to a DoD contractor's or subcontractor's business that does not take CMMC compliance seriously:

A. **You will not be able to bid on DoD contracts.** When the CMMC requirement appears in contract solicitations, and the solicitation stipulates that a particular level of CMMC is required and your business doesn't have it, you cannot bid on that contract or renew any contracts requiring it. If DoD contracts make up a substantial part or all of your business revenue, you're in trouble. Paying the money required to get CMMC compliant (which could take six months to a year) with no revenue coming in could have a devastating effect on the future of your business.

B. **You'll be more susceptible to cyber-attacks.** If you're lacking the right cybersecurity controls, it makes you more vulnerable to a cyber-attack or data theft. This obviously could have a fatal impact on your business. According to the latest breach report by IBM and Ponemon Institute based on 537 breaches across 17 countries and 17 industries in 2021, the average cost of a data breach was $4.24 million.

C. **Your reputation will take an enormous hit.** The importance of a company's reputation can't be overstated. Your customers will be more loyal to a company with a good reputation, plus you will attract more qualified people to be part of your team. A cyber-attack can instantly destroy your company's reputation. It's like a doctor who smokes. Would you trust him with your health when all the evidence suggests he's made a poor decision regarding his own health?

D. You could be fined. If your business is breached and you haven't made the necessary effort to be compliant, you could be fined or even charged by the DOJ under the False Claims Act. However, if you can show the government that you've been doing things right, your company will probably not be liable for any financial remuneration.

E. It might be difficult to get cybersecurity insurance. If you've complied with CMMC, you're likely to have all the cybersecurity controls in place that the insurance companies require. While cybersecurity insurance isn't mandatory, it's extremely important, as your business could be held liable for the theft of third-party data.

As you can see, if you are a DoD contractor, CMMC compliance is critical to your business's future success. The very lifeblood of your business could depend on it. *It underscores the importance of ingraining CMMC compliance into the culture of your company.* Boeing is a tragic reminder of how important leadership's role is in establishing the right culture within a business. Boeing had a stellar reputation in the industry and beyond before its merger with McDonnell Douglas in August 1997.

Shortly after McDonnell Douglas's leadership took over the reins, the company culture changed from "We build the best airplanes" to "We need to maximize shareholder return." Two crashes, one in October 2018, where 189 people perished, and the other in March 2019, where 157 people died, resulted from problems with their Maneuvering Characteristics Augmentation System and permanently tarnished Boeing's reputation. They were fined $2.5 billion, plus they have lost orders.

Here are eight tips on how to weave CMMC compliance into the culture of your company:

1. **Lead by example.**
   Business leaders must set a good example for their employees. If your attitude is that CMMC is more of an inconvenience than a necessity, your employees will treat it that way as well. Leading by example means listening to people and valuing their role in the company.

2. **Explain the "why" to them.**
   Your employees need to understand why it's important they must adhere to CMMC standards. They have to understand it's to protect company and client data, which keeps the business and the country safe from foreign and domestic cybercriminals. They also need to know how not complying could put the business in danger of closing, which means they will no longer have a job to go to.

3. **Continually reinforce the need for ongoing compliance.**
   With Level 1, although it's a self-assessment level, the government still might audit contractors to determine if they've met the requirements over the last year. You must have the tools in place and information readily available to show the government that you've been doing what you say you've been doing. CMMC compliance isn't something you have to achieve and then you're done with it. It is an ongoing compliance requirement.

   For businesses requiring Level 2, CMMC certification will be up for renewal every three years. At meetings, in conversations and in company literature, stress the ongoing need to adhere to the CMMC standards. Ingrain it into the mindset of your employees so it becomes second nature to them.

4. **Use positive reinforcement.**
   Congratulate people when they do things right. If it makes sense, reward them for being a great example for the team.

5. **Stress the need for ongoing compliance in the hiring process.**
   Stress the importance of CMMC in the hiring process, so it's ingrained in new employees from the very start.

6. **Use plain English.**
   Not all employees are technical. Make sure you break down the rules and procedures into plain English for them so they're easy to follow.

7. **Do it slowly.**
   It's easy for people to feel overwhelmed and suffer from information overload. Don't overload people with too much information all at once or they may never understand what's required of them.

8. **Get everyone involved.**
   Every employee must understand the importance of CMMC compliance and know what's required of them. It only takes one click by one employee to activate malware and a potential ransomware attack within your business.

One mistake you don't want to make is putting off becoming CMMC compliant. Currently, DoD expects the rulemaking process will be completed in March 2023, followed by a 60-day public comment period. DoD expects to release an interim rule to add CMMC into some new contracts as soon as rulemaking is complete. After the 60-day public comment period is completed, we can expect that CMMC requirements will begin showing up in all new contracts and contract renewals. However, nothing is set in stone, so we could still have some unexpected developments.

From the destruction and theft of data to lost productivity and reputational damage and ransomware attacks, cybercrime can destroy your business if you're not prepared. CMMC compliance is an effective, well-thought-out series of practices and controls that will protect your business and our country from foreign or domestic cybercriminals.

About John

John Hill is the founder and CEO of TechSage Solutions, one of the first Managed Services Providers in the country to become trained and certified as a Cybersecurity Maturity Model Certification (CMMC) Registered Practitioner. TechSage Solutions is a top IT company serving small to medium-sized Department of Defense (DoD) contractors in Texas. They are also a Microsoft Silver Competency Partner for small and mid-market cloud solutions. John and his team pride themselves on their deep understanding of the DoD industry and their responsive customer service.

John's mission is to help your business maintain secure and reliable systems and practices that will keep your company and data safe from cyber-attacks. As a retired military member and a former DoD contractor, John is passionate about helping businesses that the United States DoD relies on for products and services that keep our country safe from foreign adversaries. John is so ardent about the importance of cybersecurity and CMMC certification that it drove him to develop a custom process to guide DoD contractors to complete their CMMC certification and prepare them for future audits and renewals so they can get and remain compliant.

Before starting TechSage, John served in the US Air Force for 28 years. During his military tenure, he was involved with numerous advances in technology, including installing the first computer network at the Air National Guard on Lackland Air Force Base; leading the team that installed the first Internet firewall at Kelly Air Force Base; being part of the Florida-based Space Shuttle Contingency Communications team, where he provided emergency communication for recovery teams in case a shuttle launch had to abort; and running the Base Network Control Center at Kelly Air Force Base during Desert Storm.

For five years, as a DoD contractor, John managed the network for a DoD agency, keeping them safe from cyberthreats. After receiving his Bachelor of Science degree from the University of Texas at San Antonio, he started TechSage Solutions in 2000. While originally focusing on infrastructure wiring and installing servers and network systems, the company soon moved on to improving businesses' computer and network security. In 2006, TechSage Solutions became an MSP.

John is a past president of the San Antonio Chapter of the International Association of Microsoft Channel Partners and a past chairman of the board for the South Texas Emerging Technology Fund Regional Board. John is a co-author of the Amazon bestseller, Why Your Business Must Have Cybersecurity Risk Assessments, and frequently hosts webinars and seminars about information technology and cybersecurity-related topics. He also provides weekly cybersecurity-related tips through his "My Thoughts from the Deck" video posts on Vimeo, YouTube, LinkedIn, and Facebook.

John and his wife, Beth, enjoy reading, traveling, kayaking, hiking, gardening and entertaining in their backyard. They have one daughter, Lema, four grandkids, three great-grandkids and four dogs.

For more information, contact John at TechSage Solutions:
- -mail: jhill@techsagesolutions.com
- Phone: 210-582-5814
- Web: techsagesolutions.com

CHAPTER 9

HOW TO ENSURE YOU HAVE EXACTLY THE RIGHT COMPLIANCE STRATEGY WITHOUT OVERSPENDING
WHAT YOU DON'T KNOW REALLY CAN HURT YOU

BY KEVIN MANN,
President - Resilient IT

Your relationship with your child is similar to how I view CMMC 2.0 compliance. With a new baby, you must feed it because a baby can't eat on its own. You have to clothe it because a baby can't dress itself...and so on. While the role you play in your child's life as they get older is less, you still oversee what your child is doing and offer them guidance should they veer off the right path. All the while, if a problem occurs along the way, you have Child Protective Services in the background, keeping you in check. But if you do things right, the result is happiness and peace of mind.

Just like raising a child, CMMC 2.0 compliance is more work at the beginning. Plus, it's something you should always be involved with to make sure you're on the proper track – if you don't, the Cyber AB (the official Accreditation Body of the CMMC ecosystem) is looming in the background, making sure you do everything they expect you to do. But if you do things right, the result is happiness and peace of mind.

So, how do you get that state of bliss and peace of mind when it comes to CMMC 2.0 compliance? French philosopher Claude Lévi-Strauss once said, "An expert knows all the answers if you ask the right questions." What he's essentially saying is that nobody is an expert in everything. So, the first thing you must accept and acknowledge is that you don't know as much as those people who have been trained in the ins and outs of CMMC 2.0 compliance – nor should you. Your goal as a business is to market and sell your product and/or service, not to become the leading expert on CMMC 2.0 compliance.

To help you develop the best compliance strategy (and save you time and money), I've put together eight tips to help guide you along the way:

1) **Have a positive attitude.**

One of my favorite quotes about attitude is by American writer and lecturer Dale Carnegie, who said, "The only disability in life is a bad attitude." You need to adopt the right attitude toward compliance. If you don't, the results could be costly. For example, one of my IT clients (they do work for the government and have a complex computing environment) would always check all the right boxes and say they were National Institute of Standards and Technology Special Publication (NIST SP) 800-171 compliant.

They suffered a cyber-attack. All their computers and data were compromised. They had a backup, but it was from a year ago, so they lost a full year's worth of data. The only thing we were able to salvage fully was their mail system because there was a second backup for it. Their entire staff did very little during the two weeks it took things to be recovered and restored. It was a ransomware attack, which I advised them not to pay because once you pay, you become an even bigger target for hackers down the road. Before, they didn't want to spend the money on third-party assessments. Their attitude had been "We're small potatoes. Nobody cares about us."

After the attack, money became no object. They put new systems in place, and they started documenting everything. Had they been taking compliance more seriously from the start, it would have cost them way less in frustration, insurance, money, labor, time and the inconvenience and cost of losing almost all their data. It's all about attitude. If you have a positive attitude, you will always come out on top.

2) You are a target.

It's important to recognize that you're a target—if not right now, then somewhere down the road. No business is immune. It's not that cyberhackers are so smart (they've been using the same techniques for years), but many businesses simply do a poor job defending against them. If your mentality is, "I'm not worried; we're not going to be attacked; nobody cares about us; we're too small," you should change it immediately to, "I know hackers are going to attack us. I'm going to do everything in my power to stop them from succeeding."

3) Compliance is an ongoing journey, not a onetime event.

Compliance is not something you "set and forget." You must stay compliant. You must constantly review everything and be able to prove that you're doing what you're supposed to be doing.

4) Don't take self-assessment lightly.

Before CMMC 2.0, NIST SP 800-171 was the standard companies had to adhere to. As with CMMC 2.0 Level 1 (and a tiny subset of Level 2), they were not required to have a third party validate their attestation. However, what many companies did was simply check the boxes on the self-assessment form without implementing the required controls and practices. Until CMMC 2.0, there's never been a requirement for a third-party organization to come in and validate a company's NIST 800-171 self-assessment claims.

A company would download the form and answer the questions with the comfort of knowing that, most likely, no one was going to hold their answers to account. However, when it came to their Supplier Performance Risk System score, which was generated from the information they submitted, many businesses didn't realize it's almost impossible to get a perfect score of 110 initially.

Those companies increased their chances substantially of having the government knock on their door and ask them to justify their perfect score. They could have saved labor costs, time, and money by doing it right the first time. If you need CMMC 2.0 Level 1 certification, don't take it lightly. I strongly advise you to consider engaging a qualified third-party company to help you make sure you're meeting all the requirements.

5) **Be wary of "policies-and-procedures" templates.**

Often a business will find a cookie-cutter policies-and-procedures template on the Internet, slap their logo and name on it, and say, "Okay, here's our policy." Sometimes they do so without even reading the document. To avoid wasting money, talk to someone with CMMC expertise before buying a policies-and-procedures template randomly on the Internet.

You must make sure the policies and procedures are understandable, functional and align with your business. Your procedures must reflect how you execute your policies. Plus, you must continually review your policies and procedures and update them at least once a year, tracking each time you revise your policies-and-procedures document. You can't just assume you're good – you must be able to prove it. If you can't prove it, you could fail your certification.

6) Don't build your computer infrastructure as an afterthought.

When many businesses build their infrastructure, they think only of the result. They don't think about how their computer environment should be structured and set up to reduce their cyber-risk and streamline compliance. As a result, they end up with a robust system that nobody knows how to operate or what roles people need to play when it comes to security.

You must take the time to design everything right from the start and consider things such as "Where will our data live?" "Who should have access to it?" "Who needs access and to what?" "What does our sensitive data flow look like?" "How will we authenticate and using what methods?" "Is there a single point of failure or a layered approach?" "Should we use on-prem only, cloud only or a hybrid?" "Is your system security plan accurate and current?" Retrofitting after you've implemented is a painful process. It takes time and the right resources and know-how to go back and document everything.

7) Consider the cost of not doing things right.

There are two kinds of costs to consider: the hard costs and the soft costs. One hard cost of not doing things right the first time is you'll have to pay for another assessment. Other hard costs are the costs associated with a cyber-attack, such as loss of data, downtime and ransomware demands. Plus, you won't be able to bid on any DoD contracts until you become compliant (which could take six months to a year or more, depending on how much needs to be done). And then there are the soft costs, which many times people simply don't consider.

These are things you can't put a price on, such as finding

out too late that you've been doing things wrong, having to guess at something, knowing that if you're wrong, you could potentially put your company and your country at risk, not to mention ending up with a damaged company reputation.

8) Engage a Certified CMMC Professional (CCP) and Registered Practitioner Organization (RPO).

As mentioned above, it makes sense to engage a third-party consulting company to come in and help you obtain CMMC 2.0 Level 1 certification because it gives you the comfort that you've done things right and you're not going to have any problems down the road. It's also essential to engage a third-party company that has completed Certified CMMC Professional training and a CMMC RPO if you need to be compliant with CMMC 2.0 Level 2. They'll do a readiness assessment (sometimes called a preassessment or GAP assessment), which will tell you where you are, what you have, where you need to be and what you need to do to become compliant.

Qualified third-party companies know what the CMMC Third-Party Assessor Organizations (C3PAOs) are looking for and they can make sure you have all the documents required that prove you are adhering to the CMMC 2.0 compliance specifications. Having a C3PAO do an assessment costs money. You don't want to fail an assessment and spend more money on another assessment down the road. To give your company the best chance of passing an assessment on the first try, you need to engage with a CMMC 2.0 CCP trained – and ideally certified – individual and RPO that will remove the uncertainty and give you an unbiased view of exactly what you need to do.

If you don't want to hire a third-party company, you can buy a tool and do it yourself. However, the government often puts things in a way that only they understand. Only someone well-versed in CMMC 2.0 can bring clarity to what the government is asking for and what you need to do to satisfy their requirements.

Greek philosopher Socrates once said, "The only true wisdom is in knowing you know nothing." Socrates (according to his student Plato) also said, "I know that I know nothing." The point Socrates was making is that there is wisdom in acknowledging that "you don't know what you don't know." It applies to almost everything in life and is especially appropriate when it comes to CMMC certification, making my last point all the more pertinent.

Most people think being compliant is just about technology. It's not. It's about people, process, and technology. The process is the hardest part. The people (and their expertise) are the most important part because they're responsible for the process.

Use as many of the above tips as you can, and you'll save money and avoid overspending during your CMMC 2.0 compliance journey. Plus, you'll have the peace of mind of knowing you're doing your part to protect your business (and your clients' data) from people who get up in the morning with the sole intent of doing you harm.

About Kevin

Kevin Mann is the President of Resilient IT. Founded in 2017 (under the name Quad M Tech and rebranded in late 2022), Resilient IT is an MSP that serves the Northern Virginia and Washington, DC Metro areas. At the tail end of 2019, Kevin, who has been in the technology business for over two decades, shifted his business's primary focus to helping companies that do business with the Department of Defense (DoD) become Cybersecurity Maturity Model Certification (CMMC) compliant. He recognized that faced with what's required to become CMMC compliant, businesses that have never previously been scrutinized or assessed might be experiencing a bit of culture shock.

In January 2020, Kevin started his education journey to become an expert on CMMC compliance. While money is important because a business can't survive without it, Kevin's primary motivation for focusing on CMMC compliance is inspired by his desire to help keep the United States of America safe from foreign cyber-invaders. He knows there's a lot of confusion out there and is deeply committed to helping businesses understand the exact steps they need to take to keep their business, client data, and country safe.

Kevin is not an MSP owner who only knows how to run a business and has never gotten his hands dirty. (Although since 2017, his revenue has grown by 25% to 50% every year under his tutelage.) In 1995, Kevin started in an entry-level help desk position for a tech company. Over the years, he's worked his way up in the industry through hard work and an unquenchable thirst for knowledge, working for a three-person business, a large enterprise organization, and everything in between. He's been an independent consultant, subcontractor, employee, partner, and owner, and he's worked for government organizations in their IT department and for companies, such as AOL and Fannie Mae. Kevin also founded and served as president of a Computer Troubleshooters' location, a technology franchise company.

Kevin prides himself on his honesty, integrity, and ethics. He's achieved consistent annual revenue and client growth by focusing on quality clients whose values and visions align with his. His clients appreciate his commitment "to telling it like it is." Kevin and the entire Resilient IT team are committed to helping businesses understand exactly where they are and what they need to do to navigate through the uncertainty surrounding CMMC 2.0 compliance. He's a big disciple of "spreading the wealth" when it comes to information, believing the best clients are the most educated ones.

Kevin participates in executive leadership programs in the Northern Virginia, DC Metro area (IoTSSA, NSITSP, NVTC, ASAE, ASCII, CompTia, ChannelPro). He is committed to helping drive the local area business community. When not working, he enjoys traveling, movies, concerts, music, and rooting for the New York Yankees, Miami Dolphins, and Alabama Crimson Tide. He lives in Manassas, VA, and enjoys spending time with his wife and three adult children.

For more information, contact Kevin at Resilient IT:
- Email: Kevin.Mann@resilientit.us
- Phone: 571-408-8810
- Website: https://www.ResilientIT.us
- Compliance-specific website: https://www.cmmcjedi.com

CHAPTER 10

CMMC – IT'S NOT JUST FOR DOD CONTRACTORS ANYMORE

BY MARCO ALCALA,
Founder & CEO – Alcala Consulting

On January 30, 2020, the US Department of Defense released version 1.0 of a new and comprehensive framework for cybersecurity best practices. In November 2021, the DoD announced version 2.0 of this framework.

Cybersecurity Maturity Model Certification was created to provide a tool for defense contractors to measure their level of cybersecurity, as well as establish specific practices to protect sensitive information.

CMMC sets a clear standard for cybersecurity protection that all companies doing business with the DOD must embrace to be allowed to provide products and services within their associated supply chains.

Now, you might be saying to yourself, *"Who cares? I don't work with the DoD. I don't need to worry about CMMC."*

Well...think about it:

What happens with just about everything the DoD implements?

Eventually, it trickles down to regular businesses and becomes part of everyday life.

For example, consider that little aspect of our lives we call "the Internet." It was originally spearheaded by a DoD agency known as the Defense Advanced Research Projects Agency – establishing an early network between just four independent nodes known as ARPANET that appeared on the scene in 1969.

Today, we have smartphones, smart TVs and even Wi-Fi-connected refrigerators ALL linked together via this worldwide network. And the Internet represents only ONE of many inventions and standards created by the military that have become commonplace, including GPS, microwave ovens and even duct tape and superglue!

So, presuming that a DoD guideline *only* affects a limited number of businesses is clearly short-sighted. More importantly, as cybercrime represents a looming, growing danger, CMMC's extensive security protections make their embrace a wise option for any business to consider implementing as soon as possible.

Because there are only TWO types of businesses when it comes to security breaches:

- Those that KNOW they've been breached.
- Those that DON'T KNOW they've been breached.

(Please note what they both have in common...)

Now, I'm not writing this to depress you or scare you. I'm writing this because I feel so strongly about the importance of this topic, and I'll tell anybody who will listen what's going on so that they're prepared. *You need to take steps NOW to prevent future disasters later.*

MAYBE YOU THINK YOU'RE NOT A TARGET

Maybe you're reading this and saying to yourself, "I'm just a small business. No one's coming after us. This is overkill. We're not that much at risk."

Okay – let's say you do get hit by a ransomware attack. You might think, "Well, no problem, we'll just restore from backup." Yes. You'll be able to restore. But simply restoring data and applications doesn't necessarily do you much good.

Consider this – when you get hit by a ransomware attack, the first thing they do is steal your files, which then gives them a powerful lever to pull when trying to extort money from you.
If you don't pay the ransom, they're going to release that information on the Internet. Or just as bad (potentially even worse), they're going to call your business partners to pressure you by saying, "We've got your data from a company you're doing business with. If you don't pay the ransom, we're going to release that data."

And it goes way beyond ransomware attacks – today's criminals are both creative and clever in leveraging advanced technology. Recently, there have been several cases where criminals used AI "deepfake" technology to mimic the voices of company executives, enabling them to fool high-level corporate officials into handing over hundreds of thousands of dollars.

All it takes is a simple telephone call and, within moments, millions of dollars disappear. These are definitely NOT the kinds of situations you want to find yourself in.

CRIMINALS TAKE THIS STUFF SERIOUSLY AND YOU SHOULD TOO

Savvy businesses today are rightly running scared about ransomware and other cyber-attacks. It doesn't matter if you're a small company or a big company, in a small town or big city, EVERYONE's at risk, and overseas criminal gangs are operating with impunity and making a ton of money.

Maybe you've been having a problem finding and hiring qualified technical help. Well, here are some things to consider after posting that job online and wondering why there's so little interest...

Russian criminal gangs are constantly looking for people to help them launch attacks. They pay apprentices $5,000 a month on a trial basis for three months, and if they're good at it, their paychecks jump to as much as $60,000 a month. Those at the top of their game can easily earn $90,000 or more per month. How can hackers afford paying that kind of money? Because they can collect millions of dollars per hour with the ransoms their schemes generate. And that's just what "employees" earn; try to imagine the exorbitant amounts of money their bosses are pulling down.

Cybercrime's literally a multibillion-dollar industry – and these companies are run just like any other regular business. They have HR departments and offer full benefits. They even go on company retreats with all expenses paid. On social media you'll see pictures of the entire team hanging out in some luxurious, secluded location, playing games, jumping in the pool, and living large.

Why not? They can afford to lavish all this money and all these benefits on the high-value minions within their criminal empire. But you shouldn't be paying for it. You should be going all in on maximizing your business's security using the latest systems, strategies, and standards.

CMMC BENEFITS YOUR BUSINESS IN MULTIPLE WAYS

CMMC provides you the opportunity to drive a stake in the ground that sets your company apart from your competitors, because you now support and rigorously apply "industry standard" levels of security. This provides you with a clear competitive advantage over anyone else who takes a much less rigorous approach to detecting and preventing cybercrime.

Another reason businesses should pursue CMMC certification is that they're going to qualify for lower rates on cyber liability insurance. By being certified, they won't have to pay the exorbitant premiums we're now seeing in these policies. In fact, some businesses without certification are paying from 75% up to 10,000% more for liability insurance.

Insurance companies are now requiring "cybersecurity assessments" for any business in a high-risk industry that applies for cyber liability insurance. I recently went through one of these and, as part of the process, the insurer provided an Excel spreadsheet loaded with 200 questions, each requiring proof for every response.

A cybersecurity analyst reviews the information provided and may require additional proof – such as reports showing that you're updating the security patches on your clients' computers. Or screenshots of the configurations of firewalls. They'll even ask for customer contracts to make sure they meet the provisions of their security criteria.

If it sounds like they're asking for a lot of evidence, you're right. They are. And you have to provide it. Because if a claim is filed and the security promised did NOT go into effect as agreed, they will deny that claim – potentially costing you thousands, if not millions, of dollars. It's definitely not on the honor system anymore. The risks are simply too pervasive and significant.

But CMMC provides a tool to help you offset and reduce those risks – insurance companies already recognize this, and many more organizations and companies will do so as well.

A COUPLE WAYS BUSINESSES CAN GET STARTED WITH CMMC

CMMC 2.0 certification involves meeting the requirements for a specific set of practices and processes spanning 14 different security domains. I'm going to focus on a couple of specific ones you can apply immediately to get started in better protecting your business.

(A).   Awareness and Training

The #1 thing you can do to get started with CMMC is to implement "Security Awareness and Training" to educate team members on the obvious mistakes that can and do cause serious problems.

If you're not constantly training people, they're almost certainly going to fall for a phishing attack at some point. We recommend security awareness training to all our clients so that their employees are aware of what's happening now in the cybersecurity landscape. That's so they can recognize the techniques these criminal gangs are using, helping ensure they don't fall victim to these types of attacks.

For example, we recommend that at least once a quarter you conduct simulated phishing campaigns, which will let you know immediately if anybody on your team needs additional training. You can see who's clicking on the phishing emails, and that way you can go over that information with them and reduce the click rate of these events.

We've found that if people aren't properly trained, they'll click on phishing emails about 20% of the time. But with proper training, you can lower that click-through rate by about half, which helps a LOT.

(B).   Identification and Authentication

Another area of security involves taking a more rigorous approach to "Identification and Authentication" with your systems and network. This is especially important as so many people are now working from home, which raises multiple potential security issues.

To help secure home and remote users, we recommend they turn on multifactor authentication (MFA) for their VPN, for webmail and any time they use remote desktop connections to log in to their work network. The reason this is so important is that with single-factor authentication (basically just relying on only a password to gain access to an application or network), if a criminal succeeds in getting that password via phishing or a brute-force attack, they'll now be able to stuff that password into a number of other compromise attempts.

But by using multifactor authentication, you can reduce the likelihood of a successful attack by 99.9%. Now, as I'm making these recommendations, I always tell clients there's no system that's 100% secure. Criminals are going to find a way to break through your defenses one way or another, and you need to be able to detect those breaches as soon as they happen. Because, on average, it can take a company 270 days to discover that they've been breached.

Imagine everything the cybercriminals can do in that time – they can steal your data and use it to extort money from you. They can harass your business associates or customers and make similar threats. NOT knowing what's happening behind your back can get very, very scary.

CMMC JUST MAKES SENSE

It just makes good sense to embrace CMMC.

Number one, you're going to reduce the likelihood that your

business will get breached. Of course, ALL businesses get breached, no matter how many controls you have in place. (Don't imagine you're immune – even the NSA gets breached.) So, at some point, a breach WILL happen. But if you have these controls in place, the amount of damage the cybercriminals can do will be significantly less. By being CMMC compliant, you're going to recognize immediately that you HAVE been breached. And that's a big deal, because by the time most businesses find out they've been hacked, crooks are already deep within their systems and doing whatever they want. They're doing reconnaissance, they're stealing files, they're capturing everything they can use to extort money from either that business or their customer's. That's why you want to find out as quickly as possible.

Secondly, another reason businesses should pursue CMMC certification is that they're going to qualify for lower rates on cyber liability insurance. By being certified, they won't have to pay the exorbitant premiums we're now seeing charged across the industry.

Finally, businesses should adopt this model because they're going to gain a significant competitive advantage over other businesses that can't demonstrate they've got cybersecurity programs that are anywhere close to being as well put together. This means they're going to be able to close more deals in competitive bidding situations.

When I speak with prospective clients, I tell them that my cybersecurity program is over a hundred pages long. Nobody else's even comes close.

BOTTOM LINE

I hope by now you're starting to see the value in "upping your cybersecurity game" by moving forward and embracing CMMC in your business. By doing so, you not only join thousands of other savvy businesses, but you'll also have the awareness, information, and tools you need to mitigate the cybersecurity risks of today and tomorrow.

And once you have the proper CMMC controls and resources in place, so that your cybersecurity program is running the way it should, you can rest easy knowing that when you get breached (remember, it's WHEN, not IF), the amount of damage will be minimal, and your reputation is going to remain unblemished and intact.

About Marco

Marco Alcala is the founder and CEO of Alcala Consulting, founded on July 1, 1997. He started with no capital, no employees, and no plan – other than an unwavering belief that he could help his future clients use technology to make their businesses more efficient and successful.

Since then, the company has grown to include offices in Pasadena, CA, and San Antonio, TX. They primarily serve mature and rapidly-growing businesses looking to have IT and cybersecurity programs in place that simply run like clockwork.

Marco attributes his team's success to its ability to lead across a broad range of competencies, including:
- application development
- document imaging
- enterprise resource planning
- customer relationship management
- infrastructure support
- cybersecurity
- help desk

It's an extensive list – but Marco makes sure to remind clients that there's no system that's 100% secure. Criminals are going to find a way to break through your defenses one way or another, and you need to be able to detect those breaches as soon as they happen.

That's why it's so important to identify someone within your company to serve as a point person in charge of cybersecurity. With larger firms, they even hire a Chief Security Officer – but if you're a smaller firm, that can run $300,000 per year or more. Because not everyone can afford that, Alcala is now offering that service on a shared, virtual basis. That way you don't have to worry about cybersecurity, because there's somebody owning that responsibility and making sure the company's protected in the way it should be.

They even help clients who are applying for cyber liability insurance. Clients provide Marco with the application, and he answers everything and explains exactly what those responses mean in terms of associated policies and technology. And if he does discover a missing security control, he works with them to make sure it's put into place rapidly.

Marco graduated in 1997 with a Bachelor of Science in Computer Science from California State College, Northridge. In addition, he has since earned an extensive list of additional computer industry certifications, including:
- Microsoft Certified Professional
- VMWare Certified Professional – Data Center Virtualization
- VMWare Technical Sales Professional Accreditation
- VMWare Technical Sales Professional – Desktop Virtualization Accreditation

When he's not diving deeper into technology, Marco also loves dancing salsa and bachata – and when throwing a party, he'll even pull out his conga drums and invite his guests to play along. Also into health and fitness, he'll hit the gym early in the morning before heading off to work. He also enjoys mowing his lawn while listening to a good book on Audible. Marco loves to travel, and he adores his children, son Mark Anthony and daughter Isabella.

To contact Alcala Consulting:
- Phone: 877-791-4400
- Email: info@alcalaconsulting.com
- Web: https://www.alcalaconsulting.com

CHAPTER 11

THE FOUR STRATEGIES YOU MUST PUT IN PLACE
BEFORE INSURANCE COMPANIES WILL EVEN CONSIDER WRITING A CYBERSECURITY POLICY

BY ZACHARY KITCHEN,
Founder & CEO – Digital Crisis

You've seen enough news to know that you are more likely to be hacked than not, but what can you do about it? Even if you work hard on cybersecurity policies and implementation, you can still fall victim. I honestly hope you are one of the lucky ones and your company never falls prey to a cyber-attack. With that being said, I want you to know the facts, so you can prepare. Here come the facts… A recent survey found that 83% of companies in the Americas experienced at least one cyber-attack in the last 12 months.[1] That number is staggering to think about. Another 2022 survey of security leaders found a ransomware attack hit 79% of the companies surveyed, and 35% of them acknowledged they had lost access to their systems and data.[2]

1. KPMG (January2022), "2022 KPMG Fraud Outlook." https://assets. kpmg/content/dam/kpmg/xx/pdf/2022/01/fraud-survey.pdf
2. Ashwin Rodrigues (May 5, 2022), "Ransomware Attacks Are Part of the Cost of Doing Business." https://www.morningbrew.com/daily/stories/ ransomware-attacks-cost-of-business

Okay, so you're not my biggest fan after I've dropped all this doom-and-gloom knowledge, but you must acknowledge the bad, even when it's horrendous. If you just try to ignore it and hope it goes away, you could be the company in tomorrow's headlines. Don't worry, all hope is not lost. You have options. Of course, you need to invest in your cybersecurity systems and policies, but you can also consider getting a cybersecurity insurance policy to help protect against the monetary losses caused by such a breach.

Many large insurance companies now offer coverage for cyber-attacks, including ransomware. With these attacks on the rise, they won't just give you a policy without your meeting some requirements. You must prove you're doing your part to protect yourself from the attackers. That makes sense, right? They aren't going to give you flood coverage for a house that's five feet into the ocean. To make sure you're prepared for the requirements to buy coverage, I'll discuss some things you'll need to have in place.

THE STARTING LINEUP

Insurance companies are going to vary on requirements; however, there are some common ones you will see for many policies. The first one is multifactor authentication (MFA). This means your sensitive systems will require an additional step above just username and password to gain access. The second is password management, which refers to having policies around password complexity and having a safe method to store passwords. The last two requirements revolve around training. You should have general cybersecurity training and specific training to address phishing attacks.

A SECOND LAYER OF PROTECTION

Multifactor authentication, which you may also hear referred to as two-factor authentication, adds an extra layer of protection for your applications and sensitive systems and users. Do you remember the days when you handed your credit card to the clerk to swipe, instead of doing it yourself? If you do, then some clerks would check the back of your card to make sure it was signed. If you were cautious, you may have written "Check ID" on it, instead of signing it, in hopes the clerk would verify you are the person holding the card. We all know it was hit-or-miss that the clerk would ask for your ID, but for the sake of this example, let's pretend they were all good at their jobs and they did ask. That's the concept of MFA. You have your credit card with you, so that's like your username and password. Having to provide your ID to prove it's your card is the second level of authentication.

There are several ways a system may ask for the second form of "ID" before authenticating you:

- Text messaging (SMS) or email is commonly used by companies that deal directly with consumers. With this method you'll log in with your username and password and you will receive an email or text message with a code. You'll enter the code on your login screen to gain access.
- Push notification and application authenticator methods both require an app to be installed on your phone or computer. They send a message to the app in the form of a pop-up or push notification when you try to log in. The push notification method simply asks you to approve or deny the login request. The application authenticator method takes it a step further and asks you to enter a code into the app that you see on the login screen.
- The hardware method, or fast Identity online (FIDO) specification, requires you to carry a physical device that displays a code. You'll enter the code from the device after you enter your login details. The code changes every 30 to 120 seconds. This is an old-school method but still provides the most protection.

PLANNING FOR SUCCESS

Implementing MFA across your business can be an overwhelming task, so start small. It all begins with a solid plan and information campaign. Discuss what systems/users/applications are the most likely targets for intruders and start there. This will probably include your super or admin users who have full access to everything or are admins on individual systems. If your important applications don't support MFA, then access to these applications should only be available from inside your network. Discuss all of this with your employees to get them to understand the problem you're trying to solve. If employees feel involved, it will be easier to get them to buy in. Keep them in mind and try to limit the impact on their day-to-day. If something doesn't need the extra level of protection, then don't burden them.

WHERE DID I PUT THAT PASSWORD?

Password management means different things to different people. We'll address two forms of password management. The first is password policy, which deals with an organization's requirements around password complexity, reuse, lockout and how often they should be changed. The other important part of password management is where you store passwords and how they're accessed.

Every company should have rules around passwords that employees must abide by. It's estimated that 20% of breaches are accomplished with compromised credentials.[3] Some of these come from phishing but some also come from other data breaches that download encrypted passwords that are later cracked. You can make it more difficult for hackers to access your information by increasing the length and complexity of your passwords. Both the length and complexity of passwords are important, but if you have to choose one, go with password length. A password that's

---

3. International Business Machines (2021), "Cost of a Data Breach Report 2021 (summary)." https://www.ibm.com/security/data-breach

eight characters long, made up of numbers, symbols, uppercase and lowercase letters, can be cracked in as little as eight hours. A pass phrase made up of just uppercase and lowercase letters that's 12 characters long could take upwards of 300 years to crack.[4] That should tell you everything you need to know about the importance of using longer passwords.

You should also have policies regarding password reuse and rotation. How long do you have to wait before you can reuse the same password and how often do you have to change passwords? Both have consequences in a password breach. Even if a hacker gets your hashed (scrambled) password from a data breach, it could be months before someone attempts to use it. It will take some time to crack the passwords, and even then, they may sell it on the dark web and someone else will have to create a plan to use it. If your company requires changing passwords every 90 days or six months, the password may have changed by the time the hackers try to use it. On the reverse, if you are allowed to reuse the same password after six months, they can try again every few months and eventually they'll be successful.

You also need to have a secure way to store and retrieve passwords – and NO, writing it down on a sticky note doesn't count. You also can't store them in plain text on a file on your computer or phone. You need to have a highly secured system that requires a complex "master" password, or one that integrates with your domain user and password. If you're a small, one-person shop, then you can use a single-person application that doesn't allow for multiple users, but you still need to have one, even if it's just you who will access it. For larger environments that require multiple people to be able to access the same passwords, you'll need to invest in a more robust application that allows for multiple users, each with their own credentials, and has administrative settings that allow you to control which users have access to each stored password.

4. Corey Neskey, Hive Systems (2022, March 2), "Are Your Passwords in the Green?" https://www.hivesystems.io/blog/are-your-passwords-in-the-green

There are a lot of password management applications for large and small companies alike. Some of the smaller ones are free or free with limited features, some you run in your own environment and others are offered as a cloud-based service. A cloud service is fine if they have a strong security track record, but you should ask questions about how passwords are stored and what a hacker could do if they were able to breach the service's system. A good service provider won't even be able to decrypt your passwords themselves.

TEACH THEM TO FISH

Cybersecurity training of all types should be required at every business, and you'll likely have to prove that you're doing this if you're applying for an insurance policy that covers losses from a breach. *You shouldn't just require this training when an employee first starts working for you, but it should be updated and retaken every year.* The cybersecurity landscape changes too quickly to ask employees to take it only when they first start working for your company. For this book, I will focus on the more general cybersecurity awareness training and phishing training. This isn't just for your IT department, but for everyone who touches a computer at your company. Even if they only use it to check email once a day, they need to take the training.

A general cybersecurity training course covers a lot of topics and, let's face it, it's not exciting information for most. I can't cover it in its entirety, because it's a book on its own, but I'll hit the high notes. The general training should cover:

- **Password policy and management** – As discussed earlier, you need to have written policies and you need to make sure your employees know the details.
- **Safe Internet use** – Employees need to be aware of what to watch out for and to understand that visiting unknown websites can infect not only their machine but the entire company. They should also know the differences between

https and http, so they know when their connections are unsecure.

- **Social media usage and policy** – You should have a policy on the use of social media as it pertains to your company. If posts need to go through official channels, then make them aware.
- **Data management and privacy** – Do you have a data classification strategy to help determine what is sensitive customer data and what is not? If so, you need to educate your employees about what is expected of them and who to notify if data has been improperly shared. If you don't have one, then it's time to create one.
- **Clean desk policy** and how to properly store physical copies of sensitive data.
- **Personal devices being used for work** – whether they're allowed or not, and what the expectations are.
- **Company computer protection**, such as locking devices when not at your desk and backing up critical documents routinely.

This only scratches the surface of what all this training should include, but it will give you a solid foundation you can build on as you go.

Phishing training is worth emphasizing outside of the general cybersecurity training because it's often how hackers make their way into our networks. Phishing is when someone sends you an email or even phones, pretending to be a legitimate business or entity in an attempt to get you to give up personal or sensitive information. In your personal life, they could try to get your credit card or bank information. They'll pressure you into believing this is an urgent matter that must be dealt with immediately or there will be some consequences. They know that if you have time to research or call the company they pretend to be, the gig is up, so they apply pressure and urgency. In the business world, phishers will try to get you to give them computer credentials or click on a link that installs some malicious program that gives them access, or it might be a scam to get money for an unpaid invoice or business license.

Phishing training is all about teaching your employees awareness. Teach them how to spot a fake email and how to look at the full email address and not just the name they see. Discuss the various types of scams and how to spot them. Teach them to NEVER send a password or sensitive information in an email. You can also order free copies of a brochure on phishing scams from the Federal Trade Commission at https://www.bulkorder.ftc.gov/publications/scams-and-your-small-business. This shouldn't be in lieu of training, but it provides a reminder your employees can keep handy to reference when they aren't sure if something may be a scam. Just as you do with the general cybersecurity training, you should update and require new training yearly, and when new scams and tactics make it more difficult to spot.

CONCLUSION

We all have enough to worry about running a business without adding more to our plates. Hackers don't care – in fact, they count on you being too busy to properly protect your business against cyber-attacks. Getting a cybersecurity policy won't solve everything, but it can help limit the burden of a cyber-attack. By addressing the items I've outlined, you won't just be eligible for an insurance policy, but you'll improve your ability to defend against an attack in the first place. Ideally that's the goal. Keep the attack from happening but have a policy just in case it does. My company, Digital Crisis, does this day in and day out for our customers. We know that you can't be an expert in everything, so we're here to help you fill the gaps. Cybersecurity is one gap you can't leave uncovered.

About Zachary

Zachary Kitchen is the CEO of Digital Crisis, a company he founded in 2005 in Houston, TX. Digital Crisis provides managed services like remote system support, network management and business continuity consulting. They also have a strong focus on cybersecurity and compliance services.

Zach started out on the opposite side of the cybersecurity industry. When he was in middle school, he got caught hacking into the school's computer systems. The act didn't do much for his reputation with the school administration but gave him stunning street cred with the students. The news of his antics led to his first IT job at only 17 in cyber forensics with the dad of one of his classmates.

While Zach founded the company and registered his domain in 2005, he realized he didn't have the experience or knowledge to run a business straight out of high school. He went to work for a couple of companies across different sectors to build on his existing skills. Zack was working for a biodiesel company in 2009 when the recession hit, and he was laid off. While it was scary at the time, it turned out to be the kick he needed to make Digital Crisis a priority.

Since that time, he has helped over 7,000 clients worldwide realize their potential and reduced their anxiety, knowing they have someone they can trust watching their backs. Digital Crisis isn't out to sell you products or services you don't need. Zach puts people above profits and promotes job growth and small businesses in the Greater Houston Area.

When he isn't supporting his clients, Zach's not sitting idle. He leads a peer group of other Managed Services Providers worldwide to exchange ideas and support one another. When he finally unplugs, you'll find him on his bike. He recently completed a 55-mile ride from Houston to Galveston. He's also passionate about travel and lived in Bogotá, Colombia, for a while.

Contact Digital Crisis LLC:
- Email: contact@digitalcrisis.com
- Web: digitalcrisis.com
- Phone: 713-965-7200

CHAPTER 12

WHAT'S THE BEST SOFTWARE FOR MINIMIZING IT SECURITY AND CMMC COMPLIANCE RISKS?

BY MATT KATZER,
Founder – KAMIND IT

There are three principal components to CMMC 2.0 compliance. The first component is policies and procedures that identify what you are going to do. The second component is processes – the method you are going to use to put your policies and procedures into action. Your plan is the third component. Your plan maps out the activity, along with a timeline to implement your policies and procedures. These three components apply whether you require Level 1 certification, which is a self-assessment level to prove you are doing what you say you are doing, or Level 2, where the assessment is done by what's called a Certified Third-Party Assessor Organization (C3PAO). You need to remember that, unlike civil compliance, the CMMC filing is covered under a whistleblower statute (your employee or anyone could file a claim), and falsely filing information to the federal government is fraud.

A SINGLE POINT OF TRUTH

To give yourself the best chance of passing your certification and having the necessary evidence to prove you are doing what you say you are doing, you need a software package that will put the above three components into what I call "a single point of truth." This software package should contain both a document management and data collection tool that collects and organizes data and information in a way that is easily accessible and understandable by an assessor. Your business's ability to pass the assessment is directly proportional to how well your data and information are presented to the person doing the assessment. The assessor must be able to say that, from looking at your data and information, they have 100% confidence that your business is doing what you say you are doing. Keep in mind that once you file information on what you are doing, the Defense Industrial Base Cybersecurity Assessment Center (DIBCAC) can request documentation from you at any time.

PRESENTATION IS THE KEY

Therefore, data and information presentation are key to selecting the right software package. An apt metaphor is if you were buying a house. If the house you're viewing is clean and tidy, it would instill confidence in you that the owner is on top of things. However, if it's in total disarray, you would, more than likely, give it a hard pass.

The first key to selecting the right software package is its ability to present the data and information in an easy-to-understand format that gives the assessor indisputable evidence that you can back up your claims. Plus, you need a software package that will autogenerate three things:

1. Supplier Performance Risk System (SPRS) score
2. System Security Plan (SSP)
3. Plan of Action and Milestones (POA&M)

WHAT'S THE BEST SOFTWARE FOR MINIMIZING IT SECURITY AND CMMC COMPLIANCE RISKS?

The only software that meets all the above requirements is a software platform called FutureFeed. (It's important to point out that I am not affiliated with FutureFeed, and I'm not being paid to promote FutureFeed. My opinions expressed here result from hands-on use of the software packages I mention.)

DESIGNED FROM THE POINT OF VIEW OF THE ASSESSOR

The founder and CEO of FutureFeed.co is Mark Berman. Berman is one of the founding members of the Cybersecurity Maturity Model Certification Accreditation Board (CMMC AB). FutureFeed was designed from the point of view of the assessor and what they need to see to increase the probability of a business passing the certification process. FutureFeed is a user-driven data collection tool. It leads you through the process step-by-step. With FutureFeed, you have configuration options to evaluate your business against the National Institute of Standards and Technology (NIST) 800-171 standard and the CMMC 2.0 Level 2 standard. When the information is presented this way, it makes it clear what needs to be done.

Here are some other features that make FutureFeed the best software to use for CMMC 2.0 certification.

FutureFeed...

- Is designed for both CMMC 2.0 Level 1 and Level 2 and NIST 800-171.
- Forces you to upload your own policies and procedures. The other tools do not. This is important because the policies and procedures you use must be customized to your business (more about this later).
- Provides an easy way to upload evidence of compliance and activity.
- Allows the assessor to drive down on information they want to look at. It's also the only tool that allows you to limit the information and data the assessor has access to.

- Automatically generates an SPRS score, which you need to file with the federal government so contracting officers will allow you to bid on contracts. If you are using a software package that doesn't generate an SPRS score, you can either calculate it manually (which can be a challenge) or pay a third party to generate one for you.
- Generates an SSP and a POA&M, both of which are required for an SPRS filing.
- Is a living document collection tool so you can continuously enhance and update your policies, procedures, and plans, as well as upload new time-stamped evidence that demonstrates compliance.
- Allows you to rate each element from 1 to 10 based on whether it qualifies. This allows you to highlight the areas that need attention.
- Gives you the capability to determine if control owners are overloaded or have a high risk associated with them because they don't have the proper training. Level 2 has 110 controls, which means you could potentially have 110 owners of those controls. FutureFeed gives you the information you need to easily determine if someone has ownership of too many controls and which employees have the bandwidth to take ownership of more controls.
- Allows you to clone a configured environment. This means you can build out your CMMC Level 1 environment and clone the existing environment for a new CMMC Level 2 enclave. An enclave is "any small, distinct area or group enclosed or isolated within a larger one." For Level 2 businesses, an enclave can potentially save your business thousands of dollars. If you have a company of, say, 100 people, but only 20 are going to have access to Controlled Unclassified Information (CUI), you can create an enclave of the 20 and reduce the environment that needs Level 2 certification.

Of all the tools I've employed, FutureFeed is the simplest one to use. Berman (and his team) has thought through the process from start to finish and designed the tool to make it simple to manage the information in an easy-to-understand format.

OTHER CMMC-RELATED SOFTWARE

Compliance Manager GRC (Governance, Risk & Compliance) by Kaseya, works for CMMC Level 1 and Level 2. However, it is not a good choice for Level 2 because Level 2 requires software that stores data in a Federal Risk and Authorization Management Program (FedRAMP) High/International Traffic in Arms Regulation (ITAR) compliant data center like Microsoft Azure. gov or AWS.gov. Compliance Manager GRC is built on the AWS commercial product. FedRAMP and ITAR provide businesses with a standardized approach to security authorizations for cloud service offerings. Azure.gov and AWS.gov are FedRAMP compatible. AWS commercial is not. Compliance Manager GRC, down the road, will be FedRAMP compatible, but it's not today. Note: FutureFeed uses AWS.gov for secured data storage.

That said, although Compliance Manager GRC can handle a lot of data, it doesn't give you the capability to filter and intelligently control it. While an agent runs the environment and allows you to audit it, Compliance Manager GRC doesn't allow you to put the information into a form that is fit for an assessor to understand. Until Compliance Manager GRC is used in certification by a C3PAO, I would recommend going with FutureFeed over Compliance Manager GRC for Level 1. Plus, with FutureFeed you have control of updating information into the tool, independent of how you're gathering it. This is important because it allows you to easily access the information you need to prove that you're doing what you say you are doing.

Comply Up and Compliance Forge are documentation generation tools. They don't lead you through the data collection process. You could use Comply Up or Compliance Forge to customize your policies and procedures and then upload the information to FutureFeed. This would save you time because Comply Up and Compliance Forge provide you with tables that relate all the documents to each other. This is critical because it allows the assessor to quickly see what policy is related to what NIST control by looking at the footnotes. If you don't use a tool like Comply Up or Compliance Forge, you must do that part yourself or hire a third-party company to customize your policies and procedures.

Microsoft Compliance Manager provides templates for CMMC Level 2.0 and will inform you which policies you have configured are compliant. It basically gives you a compliance check. It doesn't give you evidentiary information; it gives you status information. For example, under access controls, it would say, "Yes, you've implemented access controls," and provides you with information on how it should be implemented. It's a first-generation type of product. Microsoft Compliance Manager is similar to a data collection tool, but it's limited in what it collects. The CMMC tools are still being built out. At KAMIND IT, we use it to verify the configuration, but it's not our primary tool because it doesn't give us enough information on an ongoing basis. The tool is a good start, but it's just not there yet. It's where FutureFeed started a few years ago. I estimate that in about a year they will have functionality on the level of their competition.

Some companies that need to be Level 1 certified have tried to keep track of their data and information in a spreadsheet such as Excel, but because of the sheer number of documents that need to be organized, it's extremely difficult to manage. Level 1 users need to remember that DIBCAC can audit you at any time, and the first document they will request is your current SSP. It is not uncommon in a DIBCAC audit for the auditor to call you and give you only a few days to supply the documents. The best advice I can give you in this regard is not to use a spreadsheet to manage your CMMC 2.0 compliance-related data.

DOCUMENTATION KITS/POLICIES AND PROCEDURES

For CMMC 2.0 Level 1, an extremely important consideration is the documentation kit that contains the template for your policies and procedures. Your policies and procedures outline what you need to do to become compliant. If you buy generic policies and procedures, they must be customized for your business. If an assessor sees that you're using generic policies and procedures and you've just put your company name and logo on them without customizing them to your business, chances are they will not have confidence in your assessment, and you might fail the assessment.

Carnegie Mellon University has been contracted to produce these generic policies and procedures under an open license. The school's generic policies and procedures are the source material for most of the vendors selling policies-and-procedures templates. As mentioned, customization is critical.

As an example, here is what we do at KAMIND IT. We market a Level 1 Starter Kit, which includes policies and procedures that are customized to the specific environment we work within: the Microsoft 365 E5 Security suite and Office 365 GCC High. Included in our Starter Kit is six hours of consulting time that can be used to further customize the policies and procedures to your business's environment. I cannot stress this enough. You must take customization of your policies and procedures seriously.

[Note: The above concern only applies to CMMC 2.0 Level 1 certification. With Level 2, it's much more involved, and the policies and procedures will be generated by the company you enlist to help you prepare for your C3PAO assessment.]

Compliance Tools

Name	Price	Doc Repository	Data Collector	web site
CarnegieMellon Univeristy - Software Engineering Institute	Free	N/A	N/A	https://www.sei.cmu.edu/
Compliance Forge (L1 - L2)	$4,350 - $7,395	No	N/A	https://www.complianceforge.com
ComplyUp	$600 - $1,800	Yes - AWS gov	N/A	https://www.complyup.com
Future Feed (L1 - L2)	$250 - $3,588	Yes - AWS gov	N/A	https://www.futurefeed.co
KAMIND CMMC L1 - Starter Kit with 6	$3,500	Uses FutureFeed	Microsoft Compliance Manager and Microsoft Azure Sentinel	http://www.kamind.com/CMMC-L1-Starter-Kit
Kaysea - Compliance Manager	$600	No	Yes	https://www.kaseya.com/resource/kaseya-compliance-manager-product-brief/
Microsoft - Compliance Manager	Included with Microsoft 365 E5	Yes - Azure.gov	Yes	https://docs.microsoft.com/en-us/microsoft-365/compliance/compliance-manager?view=o365-worldwide
National Defense ISAC	Free	N/A	N/A	https://ndisac.org/
NIST	Free	N/A	N/A	https://www.nist.gov

Compliance Tools Reference Diagram

No matter what software tool you choose to go with, it's important to keep in mind that you can't rely on it to autogenerate everything for you. You must pay attention to every detail to be successful. *You have to put in the work.*

I strongly believe that within a couple of years, every business will be required to have a compliance platform to do business. The risks are too great not to. Your business will be challenged to prove that you are securing information. There is too much information to not place the proof in a tool designed for data collection. Already, some insurance companies will not even consider selling you cyber liability coverage if you can't prove that you're adhering to a NIST cybersecurity framework or some other public standard, such as CMMC.

Preparing for both CMMC 2.0 Level 1 and Level 2 certification is not something a business should take upon itself. To get the quickest and best results, hire a CMMC Registered Provider Organization that is familiar with the recommended software platform, FutureFeed, and a CMMC consultant who will tell you where you are and what you need to do to become compliant.

Lastly, keep in mind that DIBCAC can audit your results at any time!

About Matt

Matt Katzer is the founder of KAMIND IT, a full-service cybersecurity firm and Microsoft partner and the first Cybersecurity Maturity Model Certification (CMMC) Registered Provider Organization (RPO) in Oregon. KAMIND IT is one of the few Microsoft partners in the country that has seven gold competencies and advanced specialization in three areas of security (only 1% of Microsoft partners ever reach Microsoft Tier 1 Gold status). Of the 30,000+ Microsoft partners in the US, only 276 are managed services providers, and only 52 can sell the Department of Defense (DoD) high-end licenses – and KAMIND IT is one of them. Their expertise level is so high they rarely have to phone Microsoft (but if they ever do, they get preferred access to Microsoft's advanced support teams).

Matt is part of the Microsoft CMMC Acceleration Program. He's one of the first to collaborate with Microsoft on cloud solutions and one of the select few in Microsoft's Advanced Programs, which means he works with information six months to a year before the rest of the partner community and his peers ever see it.

In 2017, he changed to a cybersecurity-first approach and began aligning his business with the National Institute of Standards and Technology Special Publication 800-171 standard (on which CMMC is based) for all clients, and implemented a new process, building the NIST controls and processes into KAMIND IT's deployment and strategies. The move not only reduced client costs, but it has also significantly cut down on cyber-attacks. Matt recognized early on that cybersecurity and compliance should no longer be treated as a separate division of a business, but as the foundation a business is built on in order to protect itself, its clients, and the country from cybercriminals. He's a firm believer that even if you're not a DoD contractor, the CMMC standards should be the security baseline for governing your business.

Matt developed client solutions while working in Intel's security division, where he handled problems for organizations that included the National Security Association, the DoD and NASA. Matt is a highly sought-after speaker and the author of five books on cloud computing and cybersecurity, including multiple #1 bestsellers. His books on Office 365 (over 280,000 copies purchased) are widely considered the best sources on Microsoft cloud services.

As the CEO of the largest independently owned, founder-run Tier 1 Microsoft Gold partner in the Pacific Northwest, Matt is insanely passionate about helping his customers become competitive in an increasingly technology-driven world. With CMMC compliance driving awareness, Matt views the KAMIND IT team as stewards in the cybersecurity field who have a responsibility to make sure their clients, their clients' vendors and the United States are safe from cyber-invaders.

For more information, contact Matt at KAMIND IT:
- Email: mkatzer@kamind.com
- Phone: 503-726-5933
- Web: https://www.kamind.com

CHAPTER 13

AVOID MASSIVE UP-FRONT COSTS OF CMMC COMPLIANCE WITH HARDWARE-AS-A-SERVICE (HAAS)

BY BILL RAMSEY,
CEO & Co-Founder – Soteria Technology Solutions

There's a misconception in the small and medium business market that you are compliant if you have good cybersecurity hygiene. Here's the truth: cybersecurity is not compliance. Whether it's HIPAA, NIST or Cybersecurity Maturity Model Certification (CMMC) standards, cybersecurity covers only one piece of the compliance "pie." The other pieces of the pie are personnel policies, physical security and maintaining the life cycle of your hardware (like your administrative professional's six-year-old PC).

I like pie, but that's a lot to eat in one sitting. It can also be a very expensive pie, particularly if you need to update, maintain, and replace your hardware. Creating and documenting HR policies isn't costly, but replacing everyone's PC to ensure compliance?

That can cost thousands of dollars. Still, it's necessary. The M's in CMMC stand for Maturity Model. That means you've committed to improving your company's cybersecurity processes over time to meet the performance standards of the model. CMMC compliance is not a goal to achieve, it's a continuous process of maintaining compliance standards. That includes maintaining your equipment; any equipment that's not under warranty or support can result in your organization being noncompliant.

When you implement Hardware-as-a-Service (HaaS) provided by a Registered Provider Organization (RPO) trained in CMMC compliance, you meet the CMMC life cycle maintenance standards *without* emptying your bank account. You don't have to pay at all once. Instead, you can spread the cost out over three years. We like to think of this as having your pie and eating it too.

EMPLOYEES' LONG COFFEE BREAKS MAY BE TIED TO TIRED HARDWARE

In 2018, the average age of a desktop was 4.16 years old.[1] From our experience, we know that many devices are even older. Historically, companies purchase technology like a PC or printer and then use it until it breaks or stops accepting updates. Many things factor into this way of operating, like budget or perception of need. "I don't think we can replace Becky's computer this year," the CFO might say. "We've already replaced David's and Maria's. Maybe next year." Many computers just live on until they "die" and are then replaced between every four to six years.

When your employee arrives at 8:05 a.m., they know their three-year-old computer will take five minutes to boot up. While they wait, they pour themselves a cup of coffee in the break room. After a few sips, they head back to their desk. On their way, they stop and chat with a colleague about their weekend. When they sit back down at their desk to log in and set up their programs, it's around 8:15 a.m. Suddenly, you are losing between five to

---

1. https://www.statista.com/statistics/267474/average-life-of-pc-and-tablets/

eight minutes every morning. Multiply that by 20 employees, then multiply that by an average of 22 working days in a month, and you are losing on average more than 58 hours of productivity every month. If your employee uses a five-year-old computer, they are 29% less productive.[2]

Most business owners don't realize that any system that requires an update, like Adobe or Outlook, will see a decline in system performance. Even if it's only half a percent each month, our tech experts estimate that your systems experience an 18% decline in overall performance over the first three years. By year five or six, computers are crawling at a snail's pace. That's a lot of downtime resulting from an inefficient device! Decreased productivity is only one problem that comes down to ineffective hardware maintenance and refresh. There's another major problem that can prevent your company from growing and, at worst, stop it completely.

DO YOU REMEMBER THE TPM CHIP FIASCO?

Understandably, it's difficult for companies to anticipate the release of necessary hardware updates. You may remember in June 2021, Microsoft announced that any computer running Windows 11 requires a Trusted Platform Module chip. A TPM chip protects user data, encryption keys and other confidential data behind the hardware. It's security at the hardware level. When this news was released, many businesses had no idea if their hardware was compliant. Did they need a new machine? Could their IT professional just add a chip to their current devices? Many companies had to spend thousands on replacing those devices or their employees would be working on out-of-date systems, putting their productivity and security at risk.

The TPM chip fiasco is a good way to think about CMMC compliance. Sure, you can go on for a while without it. But it's

---

2. https://www.intel.com/content/www/us/en/business/small-business/sme-pc-study.html

like taking your foot off the gas pedal of your business. Work won't stop immediately. Over time, however, you'll lose contracts, and your work (and revenue) will coast to a stop.

CMMC: STANDARDS WITH TEETH

With the onslaught of security breaches increasing year over year,[3] CMMC ensures all suppliers up and down the Department of Defense industrial base are protecting confidential data at every level, both cybersecurity and physical security. Everyone's security matters, from the Air Force fighter jet designers to porta-potty suppliers.

Before CMMC, DoD contractors followed the National Institute of Standards and Technology standards. First released in 2015, NIST are best practices and guidelines that protected confidential unclassified information on non-government systems. Businesses complied with the standards by reporting an annual self-assessment. They got used to it.

We've all seen cyber-attacks increase in frequency and severity within the last few years. In 2022, there is an estimated one ransomware attack every 11 seconds.[4] These aren't just "living in their mom's basement" high school hackers from the '80s. They are professional hacking corporations infiltrating highly sensitive government systems and small and medium-sized businesses. Of all recorded cybersecurity attacks, 43% of attacks targeted small businesses.[5]

With the increased severity of attacks on government data, NIST standards weren't covering it. Because the standards were checked via a self-assessment, auditors and assessors were never part of the equation. In short, NIST standards had no teeth.

---

3. https://www.securitymagazine.com/articles/97431-92-of-data-breaches-in-q1-2022-due-to-cyberattacks

4. https://www.cybertalk.org/2022/03/14/daunting-cyber-security-statistics-to-know-for-2022

5. https://www.accenture.com/us-en/insights/security/cost-cyber-crime-study

For some of our clients, that type of operation led to a nightmarish mash-up of different switches and hubs all over their facility.. They'd buy new machines and then their IT professional would go on Amazon and buy a tool (perhaps one made in China that's noncompliant), to pull things together. After several years, it's become a hellish conglomeration of noncompliant cords, switches and cheap hardware that puts businesses at a significantly higher risk of cybersecurity attacks and breaches.

So, when cybersecurity breaches became an unavoidable problem for businesses up and down the supply chain, the government needed a set of standards to hold suppliers accountable.

CMMC is a combination of three different standards:

1. NIST standards
2. The Federal Information Security Management Act (FISMA), a compliance regulation enacted in 2002 that requires government agencies to have information and security protection programs
3. The Defense Federal Acquisition Regulation Supplement (DFARS), which outlines cybersecurity standards for the DoD
   The primary difference between FISMA, DFARS, NIST and CMMC is that to be CMMC compliant at Level 2 or 3, you must have your standards assessed by a third-party accreditation body.

In sum: *CMMC has teeth.*

If you want to prevent noncompliance from taking a massive bite out of your business revenue, you need to be prepared to meet CMMC standards head-on. I've been in the compliance industry for more than 20 years as an IT director and HIPAA security officer for hospitals and clinics. After managing compliance during Y2K and the implementation of HIPAA for medical organizations, I know that internal IT teams don't have the capacity or training to manage compliance. Yes, a large percentage of compliance is cybersecurity. Most IT teams can implement 70% of compliance standards. The other 30% is entirely outside their wheelhouse unless they are Registered Providers (RPs).

The reality is that most IT departments are so chronically understaffed and busy putting out fires that they don't have time to get ahead of compliance. When you hire a CMMC-trained RPO to handle your compliancy and HaaS, the tens of thousands you expected to pay up-front becomes a lower anticipated monthly expense that ensures compliance, protection, and productivity.

HAAS KEEPS YOU COMPLIANT, COMPETITIVE AND SECURE WITHOUT THE HUGE UP-FRONT COSTS

When our clients came to us in the early months of CMMC, they said in a heap of frustration and concern, "Now I have to replace all of my outdated and old equipment? That's going to wipe out my bank account!" We explained to them that that's the benefit of HaaS – a monthly fee budgeted over time. Now our clients lease out all their machines from us and spread the cost of device refresh and maintenance over three years. They pay one flat rate every month. You can eat the pie one slice at a time, which keeps your financial belt from feeling tight, AND you are compliant all the while. Tastes good, doesn't it?

Implementing HaaS also primes a company for growth. Think of it like this – a company brings in half a million dollars in contracted military work. For $6,250 per month, we make sure that every new machine is compliant and at the peak of productivity. We streamline their security processes and handle the documentation. Employees use newer machines and can work faster with the most up-to-date software. By year two, the company is doing $750,000 in business. Still, our budget is the same – $75,000 per year. They are bringing in $1,000,000 in military contract revenue by year three because they are known as a reliable CMMC compliant contractor. Still, our budget for managing and maintaining their hardware and compliance stays the same. Their HaaS and CMMC compliance investment was

15% in the first year. By year three, it is only 7.5%. With HaaS, your provider makes sure you get regular device refreshes and never lose contracts in a highly competitive marketplace.

FOUR SIMPLE STEPS OF CMMC COMPLIANCE USING HAAS

Since 2018, Soteria Technology Solutions' focus has been compliance, with HaaS as a foundation compliance strategy. With 20 years of compliance experience, I know that success requires a particular mindset: *cybersecurity + continuous compliance*. When you bring HaaS and CaaS (Compliance-as-a-Service) into your business and financial strategy, it's a four-step process that lives and breathes a continuous cycle of compliance and cybersecurity. *The key word here I want you to take away is continuous.* Compliance is not simply a goal you accomplish, maintaining compliance is an ongoing process.

HaaS 4-Step Strategy for Continuous Compliance

1. Gap Analysis
2. Remediation
3. Maintenance
4. Refresh

Next, we'll break down each step, so you understand the benefits of operating with a HaaS strategy to compliance:

1. Gap Analysis
Gap Analysis is the part of the CMMC compliance process where we help clients understand two things:

(i). Where they are now.
(ii).Where they need to be (to be CMMC compliant).

From that checklist, we verify the "haves," note down the "to-dos" and design a project timeline for clients. Clients see which controls or standards will be addressed from this timeline. This prevents clients from losing major contracts. With a timeline in hand, we talk about how to budget compliance costs over three years.

2. Remediate with a CMMC Expert: Design Your Project Time Line

The next step is remediation. That's when we come into our client's facility and start implementing HaaS to fix those gaps in your compliance – the "to-do's." Alternatively, we help the client's IT team implement remediation. It's important to note that there is a distinction between hiring an RPO and using your internal IT team. Not all IT professionals are trained in CMMC standards. Unless they are an RP or RPO, it's not their job. That's why we package CaaS alongside HaaS to support our clients throughout the entire journey. Even if they lose an IT employee or bring on a new one, they'll never take their foot off the gas pedal.

We build a library of documentation of networks, policies and features required for compliance, all packages in one monthly rate. Finally, you will schedule an auditing body (C3PAO) to come out and verify that we've done everything necessary for compliance.

3. Continuous Maintenance That Meets CMMC Standards

CMMC requires that systems are updated regularly, all new devices are purchased from the NIST list of approved devices and tools, and employees receive training. There is no more rat's nest of cords and devices from mystery sellers hiding behind Amazon. With HaaS and CaaS, compliant tools and regular training are part of the package.

4. Regular Device Refresh

Just as you like a cool glass of milk (or a warm cup of coffee) with your compliance pie, you satisfy compliance standards when you receive a hardware refresh every three years. We worry about everything for our HaaS clients, and when it comes time to refresh, clients trust they are up-to-date with the latest.

The other important piece of device refresh is regular documentation. As systems are updated or upgraded, the system security plan (SSP) also needs to be updated. This kind of documentation is very specific to CMMC compliance and is outside the scope of a typical MSP's documentation expertise (unless they are an RPO). Having a well-documented SSP is critical; without it, your certification and recertification are jeopardized.

HAAS IS THE WAY FORWARD TO CMMC COMPLIANCE

This four-step process is not what most businesses are used to. It's not what our million-dollar manufacturing clients are used to, but it is the way forward for holistic security and compliance. HaaS plus the compliance mindset brings endless benefits to your business, including:

- Increased productivity
- Affordable monthly payments over three years
- Continuous CMMC compliance
- Reduced stress
- More high-level contracts
- Potential for year-over-year growth

Being successful as a DoD contractor in today's competitive market means meeting CMMC standards. Without CMMC, you risk losing contracts and, eventually, your business. No business owner wants to keep losing contracts because they fail to be CMMC compliant. No business owner wants to drain their bank account to become CMMC compliant either. HaaS ensures you are CMMC compliant without paying a massive sum up-front. With HaaS, you can have your pie and eat it too!

About Bill

Bill Ramsey is CEO and co-founder of Soteria Technology Solutions, a fast-growing IT firm that serves companies in Wichita, KS, and throughout the Midwest. He has more than 20 years of experience as an expert in IT for small and medium-sized businesses as well as the US Navy. Bill and his team at Soteria have always held a compliance mindset. Early in his career, Bill served as IT director and HIPAA security officer for Halstead Hospital and Hertzler Clinic during the Y2K debacle, and the initial years of HIPAA implementation in the early 2000s. In 2001, he founded The Bill Guy Technology Solutions, one of several entrepreneurial enterprises Bill built, grew, and sold.

With more than two decades of compliance experience, Bill knows that IT professionals must have a "compliance + cybersecurity" mindset to succeed in a competitive marketplace. It's what sets Soteria Technology Solutions apart from other MSPs. Soteria's team is founded on the understanding that cybersecurity is part of compliance, but just having good cybersecurity hygiene doesn't make you compliant. Soteria Technology Solutions is a Registered Provider Organization that employs expert Registered Providers trained to offer high-level consultation and advice to clients working to achieve CMMC compliance and retain competitive Department of Defense contracts. As an RPO, the team at Soteria Technology Solutions helps clients implement security best practices across their company in a timely and cost-efficient manner. Bill's ongoing mission is to give clients the tools they need today to grow tomorrow.

Bill was a two-time finalist for the Chamber Small Business of the Year and was awarded the *SBA Small Business Person of the Year for Kansas*. After surviving two strokes by the time he was 33 years old due to a congenital heart condition, Bill knows the value of living every day to the fullest. He serves in several local civic organizations, enjoys spending time with his wife and five children, and is passionate about traveling and absorbing the vibrant traditions, food and landscapes of cultures across the globe. Of the seven continents, he's been to six. While he finalizes plans to get to Antarctica, the last remaining continent he has yet to visit, he enjoys spending time going to Kansas City Chiefs games.

Bill lives by the motto "Today is the future." It's a message he passes on to his clients at Soteria Technology Solutions by providing industry-changing IT strategies and tools that keep them at the forefront of the technology and cybersecurity landscape today, so they cultivate growth in their industry tomorrow.

To contact Bill and/or Soteria Technology Solutions:
- Email: Bill@heysoteria.com
- Web: https://heysoteria.com
- Phone: 316-816-2600

CHAPTER 14

THE E-6 PROCESS FOR CMMC COMPLIANCY

THE SIX PIECES EVERY COMPLIANCE PLAN <u>MUST</u> INCLUDE TO KEEP YOU FROM LOSING BUSINESS DUE TO NON-COMPLIANCE

BY RUSTY GOODWIN,
Executive Consultant – The Mid-State Group

While handling compliance issues over the past two decades, I've discovered that you must understand the risks of non-compliance and factor in the human component.

We define governance as anything we make ourselves do. Compliance is anything someone else makes us do. Risk is what we are trying to avoid or mitigate by using governance or compliance.

I remember when the movement started to make cars safer with seat belts. When the government made seat belts the law of the land, many, many people resisted. Even though a lot of lives were being lost, people still wouldn't comply and refused to wear them.

To combat this resistance, education campaigns were launched, statistics were shared, and context was given about why seat belts are important. Today, it is a rare exception to find someone who will not wear a seat belt. Instead, most people self-govern and put it on voluntarily. It's become a habit. The culture was changed through context and education.

After decades of compliance, it's hard for business owners to even imagine non-compliance with Occupational Safety and Health Administration and the various HR regulations. However, compliance is the result of companies nationwide training their employees on OSHA and HR compliance over the years. But cyber-compliance seems foreign right now. Add to that the requirements many insurance carriers are embedding into their contracts to get a cyber liability insurance policy, and IT departments and C-suite executives are finding a lot piled onto their plates. A few years back, when in the process of tightening up our own compliance posture, we discovered our clients needed help with cyber-compliance too. While OSHA, HR and Cybersecurity Maturity Model Certification (CMMC) compliance may have different requirements or technical parts, one thing is the same: *convincing people to govern themselves.*

The importance of this cannot be understated. No matter how much money we spend on technology, there is *nothing* the IT department can do to protect us from ourselves unless we cooperate. Even if you spend a fortune to keep your company secure, it takes only one human error to unravel everything. Much can be done to improve risk posture. It will require, however, understanding and improving the human component. Globally we spend a quarter of a trillion dollars annually to secure our hardware and software, but over 90% of all breaches are caused by humans. How do we adopt the types of behaviors that can help mitigate this risk? That's what the E-6 process is for – to develop compliance as a culture and help protect us from the human component of compliance.

WHAT IS THE E-6 PROCESS?

The E-6 process is the easy-to-remember, repeatable method I use to help clients with the human component in their companies so they can successfully create self-governance and practice better CMMC compliance. It's a method I recommend repeating at least once a year.

WHY IS THE E-6 PROCESS IMPORTANT?

The mistake that organizations everywhere make when trying to get their employees onboard with CMMC compliance is starting with the WHAT instead of starting with the WHY. Author and inspirational speaker Simon Sinek would not approve! You must start with the WHY! It begins when organizations purchase stacks of hardware or software to help solve their problems without knowing how to use it or why they are buying it. If you don't know why you're buying it or how to use it, then technology doesn't do you any good. The E-6 process helps explain the why, the how and the what.

The order of these steps is what I've found to be most successful. It's important to note that if you miss a step or go out of order, you may find the process won't be as successful.

STEP 1: <u>EVALUATE</u>

You can't know where you're going unless you know your starting point. Imagine trying to put an address in your GPS, but the GPS doesn't know where you are. It can't possibly tell you how to get to your destination without that critical information.

Similarly, you must have a good assessment of where you are starting. Assessing your hardware and software is critical. However, you also want to evaluate the human component. For example...

- Do you conduct phishing training?
- Do you do cybersecurity awareness training?

- Do you have access control for who can see what data?
- How do you protect your data?
- What are your HR policies around cyber hygiene?

There are many questions to ask, but this is a good start.

You must also evaluate what you want your culture of compliance to look like and how much disruption your business can tolerate.

For example, let's say you begin working with a client with highly secretive data. It might be necessary to change passwords every day or to generate onetime-use passwords. On the flip side, for a client with a lesser security need, changing passwords less often is more appropriate.

Obviously, the first example is much more disruptive. Ask yourself, what kind of disruption can my business tolerate? How much is required for my organization to be compliant?

The answers are going to be different for everybody. Without evaluation, you don't really know where to start. Plus, determining the answers to those questions will help with your compliance requirements. A Department of Defense contractor must behave differently from a facility that doesn't work with the government. If you look at the CMMC framework, there are 130 control points in level 3. Although the CMMC control points are rather rigid, there may be flexibility in how a company accommodates them. For example, one organization might require a biometric scan or a Titan Security Key for login and another may show how a sophisticated password login, or a password vault, is appropriate for them. What's important is to evaluate the best way for your organization to get on the path to compliance.

Whether you are trying to satisfy the tenets of CMMC or meet the demands of the insurance carriers, it is important after evaluating your risk, to:

1) have the appropriate policies, procedures, and best practices in place.

2) train and continuously improve on, those policies and procedures.
3) document EVERYTHING. If it is not documented, it did not happen.

STEP 2: <u>EDUCATE</u>

Once you know where you're going, the next step is to gather the rest of your organization and tell them why compliance matters. Unfortunately, this is where a lot of companies fall short. They give employees training. They give them policy manuals to read when they are brought onboard. They give them all sorts of information and knowledge. But they stop short of telling them why it's important to be compliant. Before they will truly commit to your success, you must tell them WHY they should care about this knowledge. In short, you're telling them, "Here is what will happen to the company if we blow it, and here's what we're going to put in place to give us the surest path to compliance success."

LET YOUR EMPLOYEES KNOW WHO YOU ARE PROTECTING

When it comes to CMMC compliance, for you, the WHY is easy. If you want to keep doing business with the government, you must comply. But it's not just protecting your government contract and protecting national security that matters. The equally – if not more – important WHY for your employees is that they want your customers to keep writing checks so they can keep their jobs.

A manufacturing client of mine created proprietary software to run the machines they make. Now they not only put machines on their customers' premises, but they also put software on their customers' computer networks. The big, national companies they work with want to know what policies and procedures are in place to protect them as customers, so they now send spreadsheets, questionnaires and contract requirements that must be answered and agreed to, so as not to compromise their cyber-risk posture. This client's big WHY for compliance is that he wants these national companies to keep writing him checks for his machinery and software.

Other reasons include avoiding negative – and even nasty – publicity, and the damage it can do to your reputation when you are breached.

Let's not forget about the cost either. When a company is breached, it is required to notify every name in its database. The cost of breach notification alone averages $150 per name and can be even higher depending on the facility in question. Recently, I asked a prospect what it would cost at $150 per name to notify everyone if their database was breached. After doing some quick calculations, they said the cost would be $3.7 million. When I asked if that would be a bankrupting event, the prospect said it would, even with insurance. When everyone understands the context behind compliance, it helps the CFO better understand the need to spend money to ensure the organization practices compliance. And the right WHY helps the employees understand that their non-compliance could cause the company to go bankrupt, resulting in no more paychecks.

There are other costs for non-compliance. Work stoppage is a huge cost. Civil penalties may be incurred because of litigation. In recent years, executives and board members have been found personally liable for breaches under Duty of Care and Fiduciary Care. Lower-level employees may not be concerned with CMMC or government regulations, but it is important to help them understand that not being compliant puts your organization, your clients' data and even your employees' data at risk. Often the same computer system or network that houses all the customer data also houses all the employee data. Their pay rate, retirement plan and social security number are all information that your employees don't want stolen, but this is rarely mentioned to employees. Tell your employees that by helping protect the company, they are protecting themselves.

GIVE EXAMPLES

Too often, CMMC training is just a list of dos and don'ts without the WHY behind them. Typically, an employee who is out of compliance is not a bad actor. They just don't understand the best practices and the reasons behind them. It could be they are careless. It could be they aren't thinking. People more clearly understand the importance of the education they are receiving when you give them the WHY behind it. Because the WHY, when you give people the proper context, will make it easier for them to care about the WHAT you just imparted.

STEP 3: <u>EQUIP</u>

Now that you've evaluated and educated them on why they ought to care, you must give them the tools to be successful.

Your internal IT department or your MSP will typically have a suite of security products in place. But you want to make sure they have EVERYTHING they need, including phishing simulation training (so that employees know what red flags to look for), cybersecurity awareness training, and proper password management. You'll also want your physical security team to show what's important to protect in your facility. You must invest in, and give employees, the necessary tools so they can pass the compliance test and meet all your expectations.

This equip phase must be a joint effort between leadership, the IT department and physical security, because the employees need *everything* to pass the test you're getting ready to give them when asking them to comply with the CMMC framework.

STEP 4: <u>EMPOWER</u>

Once you provide them with the knowledge, including the WHY behind it, and the proper tools, they will feel empowered to protect themselves and the organization. Now that they feel empowered, you've given them every reason to do a better job.

Let's look at one area as an example: *phishing training.*

If all you do is walk in and say, "Make sure you watch out for fake e-mails," you've given them no resources to do a better job. Without any knowledge, without the WHY behind it, and without the tools, employees don't know what to do. What happens is:

1) they try their best but wind up opening a malicious e-mail anyway and get discouraged
2) they become paralyzed and are afraid to open anything, and important work doesn't get done
3) they say, "Screw it," and click on everything

No one should feel powerless. When you give employees permission to do a better job, they almost always will. From my experience, I can tell you that almost 100% of the time when we introduce phishing simulation training into an organization, the first time an MSP does a campaign, at least half the people or more will click on a bad e-mail. Over time, with consistent training, the click rate gets down to only 1% or 2% at worst and often a 0% click rate because now we've given people the knowledge and tools they need to recognize malicious e-mails. Not only do employees recognize the malicious e-mail, but they also start reporting it. This is just one example of empowering employees to do a better job.

STEP 5: <u>ENGAGE</u>

Employee engagement is vital to your success. The good news is that once you've gone through the first four steps, you'll be amazed at how engaged your employees are. Engagement means the burden of compliance is no longer falling on one department's shoulders. It's not just the IT department or management working on the process, you have the entire team of people working toward compliance. Everyone is engaged in protecting each other, protecting their data, and protecting their facilities.

Here's why engagement matters so much. When employees

become engaged, everything improves. Gallup statistics show that employee engagement positively impacts your organization and is an important predictor of your company's performance, even in a tough economy. According to Gallup.com, "Those scoring in the top half of employee engagement nearly doubled their odds of success compared with those in the bottom half." Companies with engaged employees outperformed bottom-quartile companies by 22% in profitability and 21% in productivity. Plus, the top quartile also had lower turnover, lower absenteeism, fewer safety incidents and fewer quality defects.

STEP 6: <u>ENCOURAGE</u>

The last step is to keep encouraging your employees. When they are improving, let them know they are doing a great job. For the employees who don't have it mastered, encourage them to watch training videos or refresh them about what they need to know, reminding them why it's important.

In addition to what the government requires, insurance carriers now require a much more robust risk posture when you are applying for cyber liability insurance. Included in this list of must-haves are multifactor authentication, password management, phishing training, cybersecurity training and proof you are successfully backing up your data – all things that will require you to govern yourself appropriately.

The E-6 process will not only help you comply with CMMC and satisfy your insurance carriers, but it will also ultimately create a culture of compliance in your organization. Once you have that, all the rest becomes so much simpler.

About Rusty

Rusty Goodwin has been helping companies with success, compliance, growth, and risk management for over two decades. As an organizational efficiency consultant at the Mid-State Group, he specializes in organizational efficiency, process streamlining, resource optimization, and compliance. His expertise is in creating simple and powerful solutions so busy leaders can devote the time and attention necessary to carry them out, and continue them as successful, ongoing habits. Given the nickname "the Fixer" by his clients, Rusty gained the moniker due to his innate ability to introduce immediate fixes that streamline processes and increase the bottom line. By bringing order to chaos and making seemingly impossible changes, he continually helps organizations find the answers.

After years of helping organizations create a culture of compliance regarding their Occupational Safety and Health Administration Compliance and Human Resources Compliance, Rusty began working as a consultant for managed services providers (MSPs) that hire him to help translate and simplify cyber-compliance risks and issues for their clients. With a lifetime certification in DISC Profiles/Five Behaviors and a certification in PXT Select™ (an assessment measuring thinking styles, behavioral traits, and interests), he assists by assessing the need and breaking things down simply for his clients. This enables his clients to understand all the risks and issues surrounding either the Health Insurance Portability and Accountability Act compliance framework or the Cybersecurity Maturity Model Certification framework, those implications, and the interventions they can make. (When clients take a good assessment of their risk profile, he finds that most of the time they choose to govern themselves even more conservatively than what's required of them through compliance. Therefore, he is driven to help clients understand the risk and context around compliance.)

Rusty also specializes in comprehensive organizational audits, and can provide, or assist with, compliance assessment, HR/safety integration assessment, data breach strategy and response, employee education and training, and framework best practices.

His mission is to change the attitudes and culture surrounding compliance so that every company strives to self-govern and develop a culture where compliance is the norm, not the outlier. He does this by helping C-suite executives wrap their heads around cyber-compliance, what it means, and why it's important for them to take compliance into their own hands by self-governing as well as understanding all the risks relating to compliance and non-compliance.

Rusty serves on the Product Advisory Council for Kaseya, a best-in-breed technology company that assists IT professionals in efficient management, security, and backup IT under a single pane of glass. He is also working with Technology Marketing Toolkit to develop a model for MSPs that will help their clients with compliance.

Connect with Rusty at:
- E-mail: rgoodwin@themidstategroup.com.

CHAPTER 15

HOW TO HANDLE CMMC COMPLIANCE WHEN YOUR COMPANY IS TOO SMALL TO HAVE A CISO

BY WILL SPEROW,
CEO - Blue Bay Technology, LLC

If you're not in compliance with CMMC, you can lose more than just your Department of Defense (DoD) contracts! Your business could be the weak link that enables cyber-attackers to steal Controlled Unclassified Information (CUI), and this breach could destroy your business's future, your firm's reputation, and your financial security. Cybersecurity Maturity Model Certification (CMMC) compliance will soon be required via DFARS clause 252.204-7012 and is already being added to DoD contracts.

Who is responsible for implementing and enforcing compliance within a company? Every business owner, CEO, Board of Directors, and every government security council member must answer this question.

Ensuring compliance with security standards is usually the role of the Chief Information Security Officer (CISO) or sometimes a CSO or VP of Security, depending on the organization. Yet many small and midsized businesses (SMBs) do not have the luxury of having such an individual due to the financial costs (average salary of $230,000[1]) or difficulties in finding a qualified individual.

A good CISO has a broad range of skills – not just technical knowledge to protect companies from security threats, but also other skills such as project management, risk management, vendor selection, technical writing and finally the ability to relay all of this in an understandable way to the important stakeholders of the company.

Thanks to CMMC, you're going to need to have a security expert on your side. Let's look at what a CISO job would look like for a typical company.

THE CISO'S RESPONSIBILITIES

There are a huge number of responsibilities in a CISO position. Some of these responsibilities include things like:

A. Keeping abreast of developing security threats and explaining them to the board and to stakeholders.
B. Enforcing these policies throughout the organization and conducting audit reviews to ensure vulnerabilities don't exist within the organization.
C. Management of real-time threat analysis and defense, including the prevention of data loss and fraud.
D. Planning, implementing, and maintaining security architecture.
E. Implementing identity and access management policies, including physical security.
F. Managing the security of programs and operating systems through patching and vulnerability management.

---

[1] Information from Salary.com for United States.

G. Investigations into breaches for what went wrong, remediating the cause and creating documentation for future prevention.

H. Vendor selection, purchasing and acquisition strategies for security-related tools.

Regulatory and compliance knowledge, college education, technical training and years of frontline experience go into the typical CISO's résumé. They also must be comfortable as the key advocate within the organization for emphasizing the importance of security and ensure everyone from the C-suite down knows the part they play in maintaining the security posture for the company.

CISOs are a unique position – a diamond in the rough, you could say. As in the diamond trade, prepare to pay a handsome price if you want the best quality and experienced CISO you can find, if you can find it. However, there are options for those not looking to break the bank on this position. Many companies, especially SMBs, don't need to have a full-time CISO on staff to achieve and maintain CMMC compliance.

I believe that, at a minimum, any competent IT department with enough personnel can get started on the first level of CMMC compliance with the proper guidance from an experienced cybersecurity consultant. Let's take a moment to discuss the levels of CMMC compliance and how those might influence your need for a cybersecurity consultant or a CISO or related position.

THE CMMC 2.0 LEVELS

The National Institute of Standards and Technology developed NIST 800-171 standards for protecting CUI data, and this makes up the core of CMMC. As of this writing, CMMC 2.0 has three levels, down from the previous version's five levels. Each level measures compliance with specific aspects of cybersecurity standards. The three levels are:

1. Level 1-Foundational – Only applies to companies that need to focus on protecting Federal Contract Information (FCI). These network controls protect contractor information and limit user access to "need to know" permission levels as described in the 17 specific guidelines found in NIST SP 800-171.
2. Level 2-Advanced – For companies working with CUI, aligns with the levels and security controls developed by NIST and is in complete alignment with all 110 guidelines in NIST SP 800-171.
3. Level 3-Expert – Designed for contractors working with CUI associated with the DoD's highest-priority programs and is intended to reduce the risks from advanced persistent threats. This is done through full alignment of all of NIST SP 800-171, along with NIST SP 800-172.

NIST documents contain guidance to companies that provide procedural processes to identify, protect, detect, respond to, and recover from cyber-attacks. Any company handling CUI is required to comply with at least Level 2, and soon all companies with DoD contracts with FCI will be required to comply with Level 1.

Today, most companies in the DoD space handling CUI (Levels 2 and 3 under CMMC) should have an active system security plan in place and be working toward full compliance with NIST 800-171. These companies are required to enter their scores into the Supplier Performance Risk System (SPRS), where they self-attest to the level of compliance they have achieved. Starting in late 2022 to early 2023, DoD contracting companies requiring Levels 2 and 3 compliance will need to be audited by a CMMC Third-Party Assessor Organization (C3PAO).

If you have a company performing DoD contract work without a cybersecurity consultant or CISO, someone in your IT department needs to be well-versed in the CMMC requirements and different levels required by your contracts. They should also have the authority to assess current policies, develop strategies to become compliant, have the authority to implement and enforce it throughout the organization, and monitor the organization to ensure compliance. Most small companies will need to meet Level 1 requirements at a minimum and only self-assess annually. Let's take a closer look.

THE LEVEL 1 REQUIREMENTS

Here is a brief description of the 17 guidelines embedded in the categories below required for Level 1 compliance. You can find full details inside of NIST SP 800-171, which is freely available online.

(i). Access Control

Companies must limit system access to authorized users, processes acting on behalf of authorized users and devices (including other systems). Each user, process and device must also be limited to only the types of transactions and functions that a particular position requires them to access.

Companies must also verify and control or limit the connections to, and use of, any external systems they have no control over, like employee-owned laptops and devices. Finally, CUI must be removed from publicly accessible systems or, if authorized for display, reviewed and processed, so non-public information is removed.

(ii). Identification and Authorization

Organizations have to identify all system users, processes acting on behalf of users and devices either in, or contacting, their network. These identities must be authenticated or verified before permitting access to systems in the organizations.

(iii). Media Protection

Level 1 companies must have a way to sanitize or destroy any system media containing CUI before disposal or reuse. This isn't just in drives, but also network components, scanners, copiers, printers, mobile devices, and even non-digital media. Whatever technique is used must make the information impossible to retrieve or reconstruct.

(iv). Physical Protection

Also, companies must limit physical access to systems, equipment, and operating environments to authorized individuals. If there are visitors, they must be escorted and monitored. Physical access points must also be logged, and those logs need to be maintained. Finally, any physical access devices, like keys, locks, combinations, and card readers, must be controlled and managed.

(v). System and Communication Protection

Any communication at the external boundary or key internal boundaries of systems must be monitored, controlled and protected. An example of this is traffic going in and out of a firewall, but that's just one of numerous communication points.

As part of this, organizations must also use subnetworks for publicly accessible system components that are physically or logically separated from internal networks.

(vi). System and Information Integrity

Finally, companies have to identify, report and correct system flaws in a timely manner; provide protection from malicious code at system entry and exit points; update malicious code protection mechanisms (e.g., antivirus signatures) when new releases are available; perform periodic (scheduled and unscheduled) scans of internal systems for flaws; and do real-time scans of files from external sources as they're downloaded, opened, or executed.

LEVEL 1 – SEEMS EASY, BUT NOT SO FAST

Some requirements in the full NIST document have links to other documents that go into great detail about how to fulfill the requirements properly. It's possible you're already fulfilling many of these, but many companies don't have all of them or only have them partially in place.

Another issue is that IT-centric personnel might not be as familiar with the requirements for areas such as physical security or have the talent to write policies or the knowledge to cover all of these areas with complete confidence. Level 1 companies will find solace and risk reduction in seeking outside help to verify their Level 1 compliance, even when self-assessing.

REACHING OUT FOR HELP

If you know you are required, or will be required, to achieve Level 2 or Level 3 certification, and you're a small business with no dedicated cybersecurity position, then staying compliant becomes far more risky for a successful implementation and a passing audit.

Once you know you need Level 2 or Level 3 certification, it's time to turn to outside help.

Most SMBs don't have the staff with the experience and high-level certifications needed to implement the NIST standards properly for Levels 2 and 3. There is also the added burden of keeping updated with the latest threats, plus enforcing all the policies involved with CMMC compliance, all while doing their normal IT functions that keep the company operating on a daily basis. Turning to an outside consultant with CMMC experience is your best bet to reduce your risk.

Hiring outside help solves many of the problems we've discussed so far:

1) You gain access to a large team of people with experience in cybersecurity and CMMC compliance, not a one- or two-person team found in many SMBs.
2) They have a security operations center working 24/7 to watch and respond to attacks.
3) Many companies are getting members of their team certified to become CMMC Certified Auditors, which will increase their knowledge and enable them to assist you in passing your audit from a C3PAO.
4) Most will have technical staff with high-level certifications like CISSP on their teams, which would be expensive for your IT staff to procure.
5) You gain access to a team that could help offload other noncritical IT functions such as patching or backups so your IT members can concentrate on the CMMC project.

Since outside experts usually handle multiple clients at once, they will probably have other experiences to draw upon to help lead your company toward solutions and policies that are industry-accepted. Rather than facing a government auditor on your own, likely for the first time, and working overtime to produce the documentation they want, your team gets the help it needs to lead this project while your IT team stays focused on running your business.

Finally, and most importantly, you remove a lot of what's known in the industry as the "bus factor." If you have one person in-house who knows all the secrets of your risk management plan and security infrastructure and they leave the company, for any reason, you could swiftly lose critical information needed for gaining or maintaining compliance.

By having an outside company that also possesses this information, you reduce the risk of being out of compliance and the expense and time of having to recover or rebuild this information under new IT personnel.

AN OUTSIDE VOICE

Any IT professional who has been in the field for a while can tell you a story of how they were asked – or ordered – to break a security or compliance rule or policy in order to satisfy someone in the company. This puts them in a tough spot. Following the order could compromise the company, but not following the order could threaten their job, pay or promotion possibilities.

Too many business leaders don't know the reasons IT "gets in their way" for security reasons. They have a myopic view toward getting what they want vs. what's required, and they don't want to take no for an answer. Even if they have an inkling about what the consequences could be, it could get pushed aside.

Your IT team must have the power to enforce cybersecurity policies for the good of the company, from the lowest tech all the way to the CIO. This is another area where outside help shines in cybersecurity and the CMMC world. They're an outside voice that can't be swayed as easily with threats to their job.

SIZE DOESN'T MATTER FOR SECURITY

Even if you have an excellent IT team now, they may not have the experience in security necessary to do the job right. Cybersecurity is a specialty where a person could spend their entire career. When your business depends on security compliance to survive, leave no room for mistakes or cost-cutting decisions that compromise your defenses.

Security is a highly valuable and necessary part of your business and should be treated as such. Look at it this way – would you choose to have the lowest legal liability insurance coverage on your company, or would you get more realistic coverage to minimize your risk at a higher cost? One claim can put an SMB out of business if they don't have the right insurance coverage, and one cybersecurity event can have the same results.

Your size doesn't matter. If you don't have a CISO-minded individual working for your company, you should start looking at managed services (MS) or managed security services providers (MSSP) to bring you up to speed.

This can take time though, so while you're waiting, your in-house IT should start assessing compliance with the Level 1 requirements and what needs to be done to get there, including any upgrades to older software or hardware that will not meet the requirements. Once you've found a managed services (MS), or managed security services provider (MSSP), your IT team can work together with them on what needs to be done to reach the level of compliance you need.

Finally, encourage and empower your IT team to speak up about situations where they were pressured to bend or break the rules for someone. No bit of convenience is worth the risk of losing contracts, getting sued and having the business fold because of a breach.

Remember, you're only one keystroke away from disaster. But you have the power to lessen those chances, and outside assistance is the right option for most companies that need CMMC certification or any other security- and compliance-related certification.

About Will

Will Sperow is the CEO of Blue Bay Technology, LLC (BBT), a well-known and trusted Managed Security Services Provider specializing in assisting defense contractors, medical practices, financial-related businesses, non-profits and small businesses with cybersecurity and compliance.

Will has over 25 years of experience in the information technology industry. He began his IT career in 1997, working in large organizations and data centers, along with consulting to small business owners. In 2003, wanting to fulfill a dream of becoming an entrepreneur, he formed Blue Bay Technology, which at that time was a general computer consulting company focused on the financial industry.

In 2006, Will engaged clients with compliance needs and added security and compliance services to his company's portfolio of services. As the IT support industry further changed over the years and Will's exposure to other clients increased, BBT morphed into a Managed Services Provider and on to a Managed Security Services Provider, serving many industries with unique compliance needs. Will is an active speaker on security-related topics in his local market and enjoys assisting like-minded business owners on their security and compliance journeys.

Will has the following certifications: CompTIA Network+, Security+, Certified CMMC Professional, Certified Meraki Network Administrator and CISSP.

Blue Bay Technology, LLC assists federal contractors with Cybersecurity Maturity Model Certification (CMMC), NIST 800-171 requirements for Controlled Unclassified Information, reducing the improper handling of personally identifiable information and protected health information by employees. BBT also provides a range of consulting, security risk assessments, vulnerability scans, penetration tests, digital forensics, incident response, business continuity and disaster recovery solutions.

BBT serves customers in both the public and private sectors across a variety of vertical lines of business. Their expertise enables them to help clients navigate the requirements of their specific industry to find a solution that meets their needs.

BBT is a well-known and trusted Managed Security Services Provider that specializes in assisting Department of Defense contractors, medical/health care practices and financial/real estate firms with security and compliance, including:

- CMMC/NIST for defense contractors
- FOCI for defense contractors with foreign ownership
- PCI-DSS for credit card processing
- HIPAA for patient health information
- HITECH for electronic medical records
- GDPR for privacy
- Gramm-Leach-Bliley Act for confidential financial information

For more information about Will Sperow and Blue Bay Technology (CMMC or other security consulting services or a free risk assessment), contact:

- Blue Bay Technology, LLC,
  4451 Brookfield Corporate Drive, Suite 100,
  Chantilly, VA 20151
- Phone: 703-261-7200
- Email: wsperow@bluebaytechnology.com
- Web: https://www.bluebaytechnology.com/

CHAPTER 16

CYBERSECURITY WON'T SAVE YOU IF YOU'RE NOT CMMC COMPLIANT

BY TAREK SALEM,
Director of Engineering – RBS IT Solutions

Every second, 127 new devices connect to the Internet. By 2025, it's estimated there will be 75 billion Internet-connected devices globally.[1] We're talking about your microwave, watch, speakers, PCs, thermostats, toasters, refrigerators, and toilets. Even consumer products like a cat's litter box and flip-flops are manufactured with "smart" capabilities. Technology is reshaping how humans eat, work, entertain ourselves, care for our pets and put on our deodorant (ClickStick[2] is a thing). You can probably remember a time before GPS on our phones and cars. But can you imagine life without it today? I'd prefer not to, or I'd end up halfway up a mountain with a flat tire and no snacks.

Our culture is shaped around technology. Increasingly, so is our work. Think about the ways technology helped businesses adjust to a remote work culture during the Covid-19 pandemic. Thanks

1. https://www.statista.com/statistics/802690/worldwide-connected-devices-by-access-technology/
2. https://www.kickstarter.com/projects/1317482922/clickstick-the-worlds-first-smart-deodorant-applic

to VPNs and remote workstations, employees are productive from the relative safety of their home offices or dining tables. The problem is that the way businesses *strategize* around technology hasn't changed, relative to our new work cultures. We all have the gadgets, the firewalls, and servers. We run down a cybersecurity checklist and think that the more boxes we check, the more secure we are. The problem is that purchasing the latest software is not what protects you. It's how *people* use technology as part of their business strategy that keeps them secure from cyber-attacks.

Cybersecurity must be a company-wide culture of tools, processes, and behaviors. CMMC compliance helps companies create a *mindset* and culture around cybersecurity, and that's how I encourage you to think about it. If you don't, cybersecurity tools won't save you from the consequences of human error and losing your Department of Defense (DoD) contracts.

CYBERSECURITY COMPLIANCE IS A CULTURE, NOT JUST TOOLS

The truth is that cybersecurity tools are only as good as the people who leverage them correctly. Think of your business as a road trip from Kansas City to the Grand Canyon. The Grand Canyon represents where you want to be – landing big contracts, growth, and business success. But to get there, you must navigate through three states, 15 hours on the road, and vehicle maintenance (e.g., fuel). If you don't think ahead and plan accordingly, you'll run out of gas, get lost and worst case, never make it to your destination.

You have a few tools that keep you safe while you're driving. One of the most essential tools during your 15-hour road trip is your GPS. It tells you where to go and updates regularly, based on user data – if there's an accident up ahead, if a gas station is nearby – and provides detours around construction. It gets you to where you want to go faster and safer. Cybersecurity tools are your bag of tricks. They're great! But they're not the only things that matter. Going through the compliance process helps you strategize around behaviors. You think through the possible scenarios and have a cybersecurity mindset, so you can leverage your tools effectively.

Compliance is that you remembered to put a map in the glove compartment for when your GPS fails to get a connection when you're forced to take a detour around an accident on the interstate in the middle of remote Colorado. It's why you remembered to check that you had the spare tire, lug nut wrench and jack stowed away in the trunk. It's even the tote bag of Doritos, salted peanuts and Twizzlers in the back seat for when it takes AAA four hours to get to you (because you don't actually know how to change a tire), and you have two kids in the back screaming, "Are we there yet? I'm hungry!"

Compliance is your behavior. It's the way you plan and prepare to get from A to B, detecting issues along the way and having tools to mitigate problems. It also means you've created buy-in with other people involved in the journey, because their behaviors matter too. Having a safe and successful road trip means being in a particular mindset where you hope for the best and plan for the worst. You trust it's going to go well but verify the procedures in place if it doesn't.

When you have a plan that adjusts with you over time, you've created a culture of compliance, not just a checklist of bank account–depleting demands. You can focus on what's ahead – towering mountains along the open road and your family's smiles in the rearview mirror. That's how effective CMMC compliance feels: the potential for year-over-year growth by securing big contracts and never missing a beat due to cyber-attacks. Next, we'll explain in more concrete terms what having a compliance mindset means for your business – and what happens if you don't have one.

HOW THE MATURITY MODEL WORKS

In the world of Cybersecurity Maturity Model Certification (CMMC), the future is in the maturity model. Maturity, in this sense, doesn't mean it ages into wisdom. It means you have a growth mindset of completing CMMC controls one level at a time. You complete Level 1. Do a little more, and you're at Level 2. Your employees are following along, and your business is landing big contracts and high-quality clients because you have a culture of compliance supported by practical tools and behaviors.

At RBS IT Solutions, we describe this way of thinking as a *posture*. This is everything from understanding your vulnerabilities and weak points to the controls, processes, and policies you have in place to handle cyber-attacks. It includes your business's ability to identify and mitigate attacks and how well you are poised to recover from the attack. It's the mindset that leadership and staff have around effective cybersecurity policies so you can advance to the next stage of cybersecurity compliance.

WHY CYBERSECURITY WON'T SAVE YOU

As the Director of Engineering at RBS IT Solutions, with 10 years of my career devoted to developing cybersecurity expertise, how can I say that cybersecurity won't save you? There are two significant reasons I explain to clients that highlight why cybersecurity tools alone won't save you:

1. Cybersecurity tools don't change employee behaviors – *culture does.*
2. Without CMMC compliance, you'll lose all your DoD contracts and eventually much of your business revenue.

Many businesses think cybersecurity is a checklist of tools you either have or don't have. If you have them, you are secure. If you don't, you're not protected. This mindset is why CMMC standards exist. Tools and checklists won't keep you completely safe when someone wants your data. Even a Level 1 CMMC certification requires employees to follow specific password requirements and cloud data storage controls.

Trust me, someone wants your data, and they've built a career out of trying to get it. For example, even if you have the toughest antivirus software on the market, it won't stop a criminal from pretending to be your company's CEO and tricking your employee into sending them confidential employee or customer data. In 2016, payroll details of current and past Snapchat employees were exposed during a data breach.[3] This breach was caused by a cybercriminal who pretended to be the company's CEO, Evan Spiegel, and convinced an employee to email the information. I bet you the $1 billion-net-worth company has top-tier cybersecurity software. But employee behavior is what caused the breach. CMMC addresses issues like this by requiring proof of regular employee training; it's one of the standards (controls).

ONLY AS STRONG AS YOUR WEAKEST EMPLOYEE

In a *Forbes* article, Christian Espinosa writes, "When it comes to cybercriminal activity, you're only as strong as your weakest employee."[4] Think about that for a moment. Even if you pay thousands of dollars for cybersecurity tools, your employee can bypass your most robust antivirus by responding to a simple email from a criminal posing as the company CEO (maybe you). They give away confidential information without realizing their mistake. Boom, you're like the Snapchat CEO apologizing to 700 current and former employees whose data was stolen. According to a Boston Consulting Group report on major data breaches, only 23% were caused by unsatisfactory security technology. The bulk of the breaches (77%) were caused by organizational failure, process failure or human error. All of these are based on behaviors. A security tool can't force your HR manager to follow the offboarding process promptly, so former employee accounts are removed from sensitive systems and email accounts. A compliance culture encourages positive cybersecurity behaviors because it's baked into the process.

---

3. https://www.redteamsecure.com/blog/urgent-requests-what-you-need-to-know-about-bec-scams
4. https://www.forbes.com/sites/forbestechcouncil/2021/06/25/cyber-security-is-a-culture-not-a-product/

The Institute of Electrical and Electronics Engineers, the world's largest technical professional organization, explains that many companies have invested in tools like VPNs but have largely neglected the "humanistic side" of cybersecurity, ultimately stating that this method of operating has *fatal* consequences for companies.[5] Changing employee behaviors requires staff buy-in. Reminding your employee not to write sensitive passwords down on sticky notes and fasten them to the base of their desktop monitor is not something your Syxsense or LifeLock lists in their scope of services, unfortunately.

Cybercriminals know how to exploit employees through social engineering and Business Email Compromise (BEC), which happened to Snapchat. BEC is one of the most financially compromising breaches for small and medium-sized businesses. In 2020, the FBI reported a 69% increase in overall complaints to the Internet Crime Complaint Center. The reports stated that BEC was the costliest, with 19,369 complaints and adjusted losses of $1.8 billion. Compare that to phishing scams with adjusted losses of $54 million, or ransomware with adjusted losses of $29.1 million, which we tend to hear more about in the news.[6]

So how do you create staff buy-in? Like a teenager in the back of your SUV who is not super-psyched about a 15-hour car ride with her family, your staff need you to make it relevant (and interesting). CMMC compliance requires annual cybersecurity training for employees; this is a great time to cultivate that buy-in. We recommend that you work with a CMMC cybersecurity expert who can consult with you on how to create staff buy-in and change behaviors to instill a cybersecurity mindset.

How to create staff buy-in:

⇨ Customize training for specific departments, so it's more relevant to employees.

5. https://www.computer.org/publications/tech-news/trends/humanistic-side-of-cybersecurityic
6. https://www.ic3.gov/Media/PDF/AnnualReport/2020_IC3Report.pdf

⇨ Start at the top. Leadership must be involved and spread awareness about security best practices, or the culture won't stick.

⇨ Positively reinforce good security behaviors. Psychology experts say this method has better results than punishing negative behaviors or mistakes.[7]

This is how we get rid of the sticky notes on the desktop for good! For example, employees learn about compliant ways to store passwords in training. We don't expect them to remember them all. We recommend 15-character pass phrases, for example, because those tend to be easier to remember for accounts they log in to regularly. We also suggest they store them in a password manager and use multifactor authentication.

How do you make this interesting? Write and perform a song about it or let them choose the password manager – you can do it in many ways. The important thing is that you do it, because a CMMC assessor will come around and verify your controls. If the staff hasn't bought into it, that will be a red flag.

A COMPLIANCE MINDSET WINS YOU CONTRACTS, AND MORE

A compliance mindset is good for all businesses. Those who adopt it early on will be better prepared for the future of cybersecurity culture that's changing the way every business works. Standardizing the process to measure your cybersecurity cogency is essential to your health as a company. Without it, you'll lose contracts.

According to the DoD, the CMMC compliance regulations will impact over 300,000 organizations. This includes contractors and subcontractors of the DoD. But more and more insurance companies, private bodies and even state governments are developing their own standards for cybersecurity compliance.

7. https://positivepsychology.com/positive-reinforcement-psychology/

By 2021, at least 45 states and Puerto Rico were considering legislature that deals expressly with cybersecurity standards.[8]

DoD contractors and cybersecurity insurance providers require proof that you meet more advanced cybersecurity requirements. Prospective clients, even current clients, need to know that sensitive information like Controlled Unclassified Information (CUI) is being appropriately handled, whether in the cloud or filed away in the storage closet. Ensuring employee behaviors align with your security policies and processes is a minimum requirement when running a business today. Your competitors are doing it, and the reality is that you are one of the dozens of choices for customers. If you can prove you have a compliance mindset, obtaining things like cybersecurity insurance and competitive contracts will be in your favor in your state and industry.

Compliance and regulation are the future of cybersecurity. Without a holistic compliance mindset, your cybersecurity tools won't save you. Without CMMC compliance, you'll be stopped roadside with a flat tire, watching shiny flashes of cars passing you by.

A CULTURE OF CYBERSECURITY WILL SAVE YOU

When cybersecurity is a way of thinking and a culture of operating, you are regularly implementing controls, employees are following them, and a third-party auditor verifies them. This is how a culture of compliance, and a cybersecurity mindset will save you from falling behind in a competitive market, stalling growth and, at worst, becoming a fatal victim to a fast-paced technology industry that does not believe in the motto "No man left behind." If you don't keep up, your competitors will. Cultivating a compliance and cybersecurity mindset today will set you up for success down the open road to business growth tomorrow.

---

8. https://www.ncsl.org/research/telecommunications-and-information-technology/cybersecurity-legislation-2021.aspx#

About Tarek

Tarek Salem is the Director of Engineering at RBS IT Solutions based in Wichita, KS. Tarek knows how difficult a culture shift can be; he moved to Kansas from Lebanon when he was just 19 years old. Encouraged by burgeoning opportunities in the US, he earned his degree in Management Information Systems with Finance & Management minors from Wichita State University and a Master of Business Administration with Cybersecurity concentration from Friends University, all while balancing a new culture and lifestyle. Tarek knows the challenges of building a successful life and career in a new culture.

Many of Tarek's clients depend on HIPAA, CMMC and regulatory infrastructures in their companies. Cybersecurity and compliance can feel like learning a new language. He understands that it takes patience and guidance to navigate the complicated world of IT, and that's why he's spent the last decade helping clients understand the complex language of IT cybersecurity and assisting them in making the most of their technology investments. He doesn't speak geek. He prides himself on breaking down compliance processes into words with which clients can easily engage. As Director of Engineering, Tarek manages a team of engineers who do the same for clients. Having honest and understandable conversations, the team at RBS IT Solutions assists clients in maintaining their IT environments and designing expert proactive cybersecurity solutions.

Tarek is a proud father to his toddler son and enjoys spending time with his wife and young family in their Kansas community. They enjoy visiting local breweries and visiting family and friends.

Here's how you can get touch with Tarek at RBS IT Solutions:
- Email: tsalem@rbsitsolutions.com
- Phone: 316-247-8016
- Web: https://www.rbsitsolutions.com/

CHAPTER 17

HOW TO HANDLE CYBERSECURITY AND CMMC COMPLIANCE WITHOUT AN INTERNAL IT DEPARTMENT

BY TIMOTHY POYNER,
President – Creative Technology Solutions, Inc.

What has been will be again,
and what has been done will be done again;
there is nothing new under the sun.
– Ecclesiastes 1:9

According to this verse from the Old Testament, there's nothing NEW under the sun. But it often doesn't feel that way – especially in view of the rapid pace of change we increasingly experience with every new year. This is certainly the case when it comes to the growing barrage of cyberthreats and security concerns.

Even so, the ancient message from Ecclesiastes continues to ring true. And though the methods for ransomware, blackmail

193

and data theft are constantly increasing, the heart that motivates online criminals remains steadfast in its desire to do you and your business ill. In that sense, there is indeed nothing new under the sun.

That's why it's a very good thing that more and more small businesses recognize that cybersecurity MUST be their top priority. It's no longer a matter of IF you're going to get attacked, it's a matter of WHEN (along with your ability to recover).

ANY SECURITY THREAT CAN BRING DISASTER

Few small businesses can survive a major attack – especially if it results in an actual breach. Statistically, 60% of small companies that suffer a cyber-attack will go out of business within six months, yet 47% of small businesses have no understanding of how to protect themselves. And 54% don't even have a plan in place for reacting to cyber-attacks.

Not having any kind of cybersecurity plan is extremely shortsighted. Because if a small business doesn't have proper protections in place, it'll simply be too expensive for them to survive. It's not only the expense of paying off the ransom, there's also remediation costs and legal costs (there WILL be significant legal costs if you're hacked, no way around it).

And don't ignore the very REAL costs in downtime and the energy you'll waste dealing with the aftermath of an attack. Recovery can literally take weeks, even months, and will divert you from the continued challenge of driving your business forward.

Finally, there's the investment you'll have to make in PR to make sure your clients are going to stick with you. If you're compromised in a major way, you can't hide it and people will know (breaches, by law, will be public events). It will become a significant obstacle to trust for your company.

Put it all together, and the total cost and impact of a breach could very well drive you out of business.

WHY SMALL BUSINESSES ARE NATURALLY VULNERABLE

We know that 43% of cyber-attacks are targeted at small businesses (even though 54% of small businesses think they are too small). More than half of small and midsized businesses reported suffering at least one cyber-attack in the past year. And yet 47% of small businesses have no understanding of how to protect themselves against such attacks, and most do not have a plan in place for reacting when they occur.

My company, Creative Technology Solutions Inc., focuses on (but is not limited to) professional service firms that support other small businesses with specialty services such as legal, marketing, insurance, engineering, architecture, finance, and accounting.

We have a heart for these kinds of companies because their focus on service mirrors our own. Our role is to fill in the gaps for managing IT and security, because most small businesses can't cost-justify hiring their own internal resources dedicated solely to security and technology management.

By assisting in this way, we allow our customers to focus on those aspects of their business where they excel – enabling them to grow and prosper, without worrying about the headaches associated with technology.

For example, consider a typical start-up accounting firm. Often it starts as a one-person shop. They're focused on providing stellar accounting services, not on the tech involved with running their business. But they'll cobble together what they need, probably starting with licensing a single copy of Office 365. If business goes well, they'll add a few more team members. Before you know it, there are five or six people working in the office. And that's when it starts getting complicated.

People are working remotely, probably without a VPN. They've cobbled together a rudimentary internal network, a printer, a couple PCs, maybe a laptop or two. Since they have an Internet connection, they probably have a "modem" or consumer-grade "router" (not a true business-class firewall). They'll finagle some cabling and slap together a Wi-Fi wireless network without proper security. In order to save money, they'll typically utilize someone they know to pull everything together – a son, brother or friend who's willing to help them out for free (or close to it).

These are often the telltale warning signs we see when we arrive on the scene. Quite often we find an absolute mess that resembles a teetering house of cards about to topple over. The first step in protecting most small businesses is getting their infrastructure into some level of order – not only does this set the stage for putting a proper security stack in place, but it also stabilizes and allows things to start operating more smoothly. The result is that technology is more efficient, and users are more productive.

This gives them an early but important win. Then, once an optimal infrastructure is implemented, it's easier to start taking additional steps to address core security areas.

For example, it's surprising how many small businesses aren't utilizing and requiring good password behaviors – including using complex passwords and non-shared passwords, not reusing same passwords for multiple logins, etc. Passwords are typically written down and placed in obvious locations (e.g., sticky notes on monitors, taped to button of keyboards, etc.). This is especially alarming when 63% of confirmed data breaches leveraged a weak, default or stolen password. That's why instilling proper password discipline is almost always the first place to start.

Next, we need to acknowledge that implementing more complex passwords is not enough anymore. Even though we've been hearing this for years, we still find that small businesses haven't implemented multi- or dual-factor authentication. MFA is the natural next step to thwarting compromised passwords. If you're not doing multifactor, you're not even doing the minimum level of protection. (If you're shopping for cyber insurance, this will be one of the first things required when completing the application. Using MFA is simply not even just an option anymore.)

From here, another policy that can go a long way toward protecting the business is to stop allowing employees from using their own personal devices on the company network. At a minimum, limit access to your internal network to only those devices you know can be kept secure.

Along with good technology-use policies that all team members embrace and practice, we need to make sure end points (workstations, laptops, servers, and mobile devices) are properly protected with modern behaviorally-based technology that utilizes artificial intelligence and are monitored by a secure operations center component 24/7.

Finally, email protection is critical because email is THE most common entry point for a successful compromise. It's often through a phishing attack, where the threat actor is masquerading as someone the victim knows, where they'll use info about the person or business (usually via data they've managed to harvest already) to trick a user into doing something that opens an entry point for further exploitation. I'm shocked at how many small businesses are using personal email accounts (e.g., Gmail, Yahoo, AOL) instead of business-class email accounts/services.

In addition, they're not using any email security – there's no filtering going on, or there's no anti-phishing protection. They're not even backing up their email in a way that would allow them to quickly revert to a known good state if they were breached.

These policies are only the STARTING point when it comes to protecting your business, and are good, common-sense foundational security practices. Ultimately, a small business needs to understand that there is not a single "silver bullet." Instead, a multifaceted security stack should be identified and implemented.

SO, SHOULD YOU HIRE OR OUTSOURCE?

It's unlikely that even the most basic things outlined above could be tackled by most small businesses, based on their current staffing. Outsourcing or hiring knowledgeable/experienced resources will be required. In considering the pros and cons of outsourcing vs. hiring someone in-house, a small business faces some very real challenges.

First, because technology and the world of cyberthreats change rapidly, it's rare for the business to have the technical expertise in-house required to properly assess the trade-offs involved.

Even more to the point, as a small business, you're almost certainly not going to have the budget to hire significant dedicated IT resources. You will need to pick someone to manage your IT. For most small businesses, if they hire internally, it'll probably be a single resource. The problem here is that no matter how highly skilled, fully educated, or competent that person is, they're still going to be limited by their experiences and what they know.

While these types of hires may be good people, they can unintentionally hold a small business hostage. A single person who becomes the gatekeeper to the small business's technology information and security can hamstring the business because that one person now has ALL the knowledge.

What happens if they decide to use that against you?

Let's presume they wouldn't. Great. But what happens if something happens to them? What happens if they get sick, or worse (e.g., get involved in a fatal accident)? What happens when they go on vacation – and THAT is when your system gets breached or goes down? What then?

These are the things you need to think about when making the decision about whether you want to hire internally or outsource these responsibilities. And if you choose to outsource, then you need to figure out the criteria to determine whether you've chosen the right partner.

It's important to approach this strategically by considering exactly what a trusted partnership would look like from your perspective as business owner. What is the relationship like? How do things work? What are the results you want to experience?

Our approach at Creative Technology Solutions Inc. is to show you how we're going to make sure you get the results you desire and explain why you're going to get them. I invest much more time talking about business direction and objectives and far less time discussing the technology side of it – things like server specifications or which antivirus program you need.

By working with us and our strategic partners, our customers gain access to the most current, top-of-the-line enterprise-level tools, services, and support, coupled with "best of class" security frameworks and processes that are the right fit for them. This approach not only sets us apart from a number of our competitors, but it's also simply the right thing to do.

And while we are a technology company, technology isn't the primary goal. The goal is to help our clients thrive. The technology we recommend and help implement will be an integral part of the wave our customer's business rides to help them achieve their business objectives. It's only a means to the more important end.

THE VALUE OF CMMC COMPLIANCE

We're seeing increased interest by businesses in not only upgrading their technology but also applying security compliance standards such as Cybersecurity Maturity Model Certification

(CMMC), even when it's not yet "officially" mandated for their operations. This is wise for a small business, because regardless of the specific market you serve, applying a structured framework of best practices helps ensure your business is doing everything possible to keep its information secure and customers protected.

The truth is that, given the ever-increasing level of threats, eventually something is going to go wrong. Therefore, the question isn't "How do you keep it from ever happening?" Instead, it's "Are you ready to respond when it does go wrong?"

Similar to what happened with Covid, the likelihood is that even though prevention and protection reduce the odds, you'll be breached – every small business should assume they WILL be breached. Employees are going to click on something and it's going to open a back door to a malicious actor. It's inevitable.

But the good news is that's okay. Because if you have in place the CMMC compliance framework, you've already created contingency plans to address and respond to attacks. When you have a clearly defined compliance strategy properly implemented, you can finally breathe easier. You can feel confident that you're protecting the people and the information you care about – for your staff, your clients, and your business.

And because you've taken this seriously, you now have the tools, infrastructure, policies, and procedures all working together to prevent, protect and remediate bad activities so they're no longer able to cripple your business.

IT'S NOT ABOUT RULES, IT'S ABOUT DOING THE RIGHT THINGS TOGETHER

Cybersecurity doesn't have to be this hairy, scary monster you must constantly be afraid of. It's also not about waiting until we're required to do something. It's more a matter of putting the right things in place now so you can enjoy more of your life, more of your business, more of whatever you want to do, without this constant nagging fear that something's going to go wrong.

When we come alongside our clients and discuss technology and the best ways to ensure your business is secured, the idea isn't to hit you square in the face with CMMC compliance – "Here are the 43 different categories and the 17 different 'whatever's' you must do..."

Who wants that?

Instead, we focus on how to make compliance a more natural part of your business culture and NOT a list of requirements nobody wants to do. We apply and follow these best practices because they're the right things to do, for our business, our neighbors, our customers, our nation – for our entire community. We want to be in this together, regardless of whether we're being required by an industry to be compliant or just being good citizens.

Those are the things we're excited about doing and sharing with the customers we partner with and serve...because it speaks to something deeper.

As Ecclesiastes concludes, for those of us who are wise, our ambition should be to share our wisdom with each other. This wisdom should encourage us all to live rightly and well, even though there will never be a final word (there is no end to "publishing of books" or constant study).

In the end, it's about doing the right thing and acting on what we have heard and know to be true.
Someday there will ultimately be judgment on cybercrime. Those who practice it will not win. But in the here and now, as we are all living together "under the sun," regardless of the size of your business, let's partner together to more proactively do the things that protect us and each other.

About Timothy

Timothy Poyner is the President, Founder and Owner of Creative Technology Solutions, Inc. For close to 30 years, he's grown to appreciate the threat cyber-attacks pose and the need for increasing diligence in the application of state-of-the-art security protocols – not only in keeping customers secure from attack, but also in enabling a rapid response when a breach does occur.

Taking a more proactive stance against cyber-crime by embracing compliance standards represents a trend he sees only increasing. More and more of his clients, both small businesses and nonprofits, understand that even if they're not associated with health care or involved with the government, they're still a huge target. And the experience of getting hacked has nothing to do with the size of the business or organization. Everyone's vulnerable. That's created a mental shift toward embracing a structured approach to compliance and leveraging best practices using top-tier technology solutions.

And Tim sees cybersecurity not just as a business issue or even a responsibility – it's a culture we all must share together. It's how we care for each other and it's simply part of being a good citizen. When you're compliant in how you're setting up your technology and protecting your clients, your partners, and your team members, you're also playing an important role in stopping bad actors from getting into areas of our government and infrastructure, potentially crippling us as a united people.

Tim graduated with a BA in Christian Ministries, with minors in Church Music and Bible from Grace College, Winona Lake, IN, in 1984. He continued studies at Grace Seminary to achieve an MA in counseling in 1988. Additionally, Tim is a certified Apple consultant and has been a member of the Apple Consultants Network for most of the years of his business.

His counseling degree and people-centered approach perfectly complement his business's direction and focus, proving formative in shaping his vision for keeping people central in providing technology services.

As you might imagine, Tim's family is one of his greatest loves. Eldest son Jordan and daughter-in-law Sarah just had the first grandbaby, Henry. Middle son Jacob works as the distance/cross-country coach at Tim's alma mater (Grace College). And the youngest, daughter Karly, recently married husband Owen and is actively pursuing a doctorate at the University of Memphis.

Tim split his growing-up years between being close to the ocean (Florida) and in the foothills of the Appalachian Mountains and East Coast (Maryland). The majesty and beauty of both geographies are instilled deep within Tim and are places he and his family frequent as time and opportunity allow. Tim also has a lifelong passion for music. His predominant instrument is the keyboard, and he has served for over 25 years as the music director at his church.

Contact Creative Technology Solutions, Inc., Winona Lake, IN 46590:
- Email: tpoyner@creativetechs.biz
- Web: https://www.creativetechs.biz
- Phone: 574-268-2874
- LinkedIn: linkedin.com/in/creativetechs

CHAPTER 18

HUMANS AND CYBERCOMPLIANCE: YOUR WORKFORCE IS YOUR BIGGEST CYBER-RISK

BY TROY McCOLLUM,
Founder & Co-owner – Layer 9

The term "firewall" originally referred to an actual physical wall built to confine a fire from jumping from one adjacent building to another. The term also applied to metal sheeting keeping the engine compartment of an aircraft or vehicle separate from where passengers sat.

But as it relates to computer networks, some credit the first mention of a firewall to the hit 1983 film *Wargames* – a movie that clearly demonstrated the dangers of "bad actors" wreaking havoc.

Today, practically every business recognizes the importance of having an up-to-date firewall in place to keep their internal network secure from the many dangers lurking on the Internet.

Firewall technology leverages a blend of software and hardware to monitor and control incoming and outgoing network traffic based upon a predetermined set of rules.

No one doubts the importance of having such a safeguard in place. But there's one more component to constructing an optimal firewall solution that many ignore or overlook:

THE *HUMAN* FIREWALL

Hardware and software can go only so far – and the firewall most often breeched is the *human firewall*, composed of the people you work with daily. Because no matter how well-intentioned your workforce and team may be, inevitably there will be times when they get rushed or don't pay attention – and that's when bad things happen.

YOU'RE PROBABLY NOT AS SECURE AS YOU MIGHT IMAGINE

There are plenty of misconceptions business owners and managers have today regarding cybersecurity.

Oh sure, they all say they understand the threat and take it seriously. For example, they feel secure because they put in a good backup system. Or they've installed the latest antivirus software. Or they've attended one cybersecurity event or webinar a couple years ago.

But they fail to recognize that security isn't merely some switch you can flip ON or OFF. It isn't one more piece of equipment to add to the network or a new updated version of software to install. Instead, security represents a mindset and skill set that you must constantly monitor and improve upon. Just as it's critical to keep current on the competitive factors taking place in your market, a consistent focus on maintaining security has got to be built into the basic operations of your business.

And because the threats are ever-changing, you must be constantly monitoring and improving as well. It's not "fire and forget." You can't just run an internal training once a year and call it good. New employees come onboard; people move into different positions. And when a bad actor from outside gets inside your network, they'll ransack everything – including your HR and personnel information – to uncover which employees are potentially the most vulnerable or profitable to target and exploit.

I typically find that even though people want to do something about improving cybersecurity, they just don't know where to start. Maybe they've contracted a Managed Services Provider or they still have some friend of a friend managing their network. It doesn't really matter because they simply don't know where they stand regarding security:

- They're not sure how good their backups are and if they'll really work or not.
- They may not know what their different business contracts require or what their customers require.
- They can't tell what kinds of data they have to manage in-house.
- They may be tightrope-walking across a number of different kinds of compliance – HIPAA, FTC or CMMC...they're unsure of what any of them really mean in terms of tasks and responsibilities and even where to start.
- And they especially don't know how to train their staff.

That final bullet is especially important when it comes to creating a secure business infrastructure. Of course, everybody knows you should train your staff on security. But most businesses don't know how or even where to start. When I ask about staff and team training, the conversation typically goes like this:

"Well, we had a meeting one time, three years ago, about cybersecurity."

"So, how did it go?"

"Pretty good."

"Well, who attended?"

"I'm not sure half the people are even here anymore."

It's all very ad hoc, catch-as-catch-can. There are no established plans, procedures, or assessment criteria in place. Which is totally the opposite of what implementing a secure environment requires, as illustrated by the comprehensive approach involved with achieving Cybersecurity Maturity Model Certification, which mandates you document each step and provide proof it's been accomplished.

With CMMC, you HAVE to go beyond a superficial, surface-level approach. For example, if you run a test phishing campaign and discover that 17% of your end users failed, just having that score means nothing. What did you do with that information? What steps have you taken to go back to those 17% and improve their understanding and awareness so they DON'T get fooled next time?

POLICIES – DOCUMENTED, KNOWN AND ENFORCED – MATTER MOST

You're just setting yourself up for disaster if you don't have a real policy on what your people can and can't do on the network.

Let's say they're checking their private email accounts during regular work hours and there's no policy in place against it, nothing to block it or look at it. Sorry, but this means your office door's wide open. We see it all the time, where people are allowed to click on links or bounce around online in any way they want. There's no policy in place letting them know what they can and can't do.

These kinds of scenarios create your biggest threats. Because people who aren't educated and constantly reminded, simply don't know what's possible or think it won't affect them because "we're too small." Company size doesn't matter. You're an IP address – that's all the bad guys care about.

And people always forget about bringing their private cell phones into the office. Let's say you have Jim at home on the Internet, using his phone or device. He's checking his emails, clicking links and, in the process, winds up getting phished – so now he's got a problem on his phone. Next day, Jim comes into the office but doesn't know there's a problem. He connects his phone to the corporate Wi-Fi like nothing's the matter. Now you've let somebody in the back door. But you don't know because there wasn't a policy about him doing something like this, and his phone wasn't being monitored because it was a private device.

We unfortunately had a case where a new client's employee was working from home. On MONDAY this person connected to their VPN on the company-provided laptop. But there was a misconfiguration of how the firewall interacted with the VPN. The employee left the machine to cook dinner, leaving the laptop screen unlocked. Their 10-year-old came in, jumped on the laptop, and went to a "not great" website. The kid downloaded a random game that had malware attached to it. Boom!

Fast-forward to FRIDAY – at 4:30 a.m., the entire network began getting encrypted. By 8:00 a.m., it was totally encrypted, and nobody could access anything.

Over the previous four days, hackers had stolen the company's precious information. (And this was an insurance company, which means there was all kinds of customer data affected.) Even though they had good backups, they still had to deal with cyber insurance, forensics, legal, etc. They were back up and running within a couple of days, which wasn't horrific, but it was bad enough because they also had to deal with the ramifications for weeks afterwards. Now they've got to do credit monitoring for all their employees, they've got to figure out what information was stolen from their customers and so on.

All of this could have been prevented with policies that were clearly understood, implemented and monitored.

THE BEST WAYS TO ENSURE YOUR TEAM GETS IT

Creating a culture built around staying secure is all about making people aware and letting them know what could happen to them. Whenever I do a training, I always start the conversation by tying it back to their personal information. "So, how would you feel if, after clicking that email link, you discovered it wasn't just the company's data that was out on the dark web, it was also yours?" Because, as I mentioned earlier, the bad actors head straight for the personnel files and grab that data right from the get-go.

You need to get your managers, supervisors, and employees to understand and buy into how important it is to follow the policies you've put in place. Most of all, people need to know the WHY.

If you're just telling them, "Don't go on Facebook, don't go on Netflix," it's just more blah-blah-blah from the boss. Instead, explain and articulate properly WHY it's important for them to do what's needed – because from their first day on the job, they really are putting their own credit and personal information at risk by going to Facebook or Netflix.

These policies aren't just there to keep you from screwing around at work. It's much, much deeper than that.

HERE'S HOW CMMC HELPS EVERYONE UNDERSTAND THE NEED FOR SECURITY

On January 31, 2020, the US Department of Defense (DoD) first released a series of security protocols entitled Cybersecurity Maturity Model Certification (CMMC). Originally created as a tool for defense contractors to measure their level of cybersecurity, it has been embraced by more and more industries as a way to establish specific practices to protect sensitive information.

There are over a hundred controls that are required to be CMMC compliant. And when you start your CMMC journey – which will take six months to a year –a lot of specific things are required to happen.

The first thing that must happen is the Business Impact Analysis, or BIA, which exists to determine the overall impact on the business if it gets breached, has its data stolen, loses emails or gets shut down. Doing the BIA involves looking at the operations of all the different departments. It's a detailed, rigorous process that, frankly, many businesses have probably never even considered doing for themselves.

Next, you'll need to define the requirements for the information you're protecting – you've got to discover everything involved. And those are all part of the controls that people seem to miss. They think it's as simple as just turning on two-factor authentication or offering some end-user training, and then you can check off all the boxes.

Well, that's some of the boxes, but it's just the start. Certification requires that you have clear policies defined. For example:

- What is your wireless policy?
- What is your end-user policy?
- What is your hiring policy?
- What is your termination policy?

You must dig into all of this, and it's not just having those controls in the policies, but also making sure you're checking their associated enforcement. So yes, you turned on two-factor authentication, but did you audit it to make sure it was enabled for all accounts?

And with CMMC, it's not just two-factor they're looking for – it's making sure you're auditing those systems daily, not just every quarter or so. It's making sure you've named someone to handle the role of compliance manager, a person assigned the responsibility to understand the big picture and ensure that the business and its customers are being protected.

You've got to have a real plan for cyber-security and how you plan to implement everything, step-by-step, with dates and milestones and owners. Because what CMMC is looking to ensure is that we're following all the steps necessary and doing everything we can to protect vital information. That's the goal.

BUSINESS BENEFITS GO BEYOND CERTIFICATION

Obviously, one of the great things you get with CMMC compliance is you can then bid on contracts with organizations like the DoD that require it. And you gain by having an increased level of cybersecurity for data and your network.

But going through this entire certification process delivers a far greater, longer-lasting benefit. It means you're becoming a more mature business. You're not only protecting your customers' data, but you're also protecting yourself and your employees as well.

And it's also going to lead to an increase in production, because by going through CMMC's required BIA, you're going to start uncovering alternative workflows and things that need to be done differently.

By doing this kind of big-picture review of your business across its entire operations, you'll see things you've been doing halfway for so many years. You'll see where you need to upgrade your systems, processes, policies, etc. You'll discover duplicate or unnecessary software licenses – items you would've never noticed before but now realize can provide genuine cost savings as well as productivity enhancements.

All thanks to getting onboard with the process and mindset that CMMC dictates and supports.

This means you WON'T have to worry about that human firewall anymore – you'll have systems, policies, and controls in place to keep your business, your team, and your customers secure.

About Troy

Troy McCollum is founder and co-owner with his wife of Layer 9, which he's run since starting it in 2002.

Troy grew up around computers – his father ran a "break-fix" repair service for PCs. Always into electronics, audio, and gadgetry, from the age of 15 he worked in the family business serving people in the community.

The spark that led to founding Layer 9 came from an offhand discussion with his father about business strategy – Troy felt they should widen their focus to small businesses. Dad told him, "Hey, son, if you think it's that easy, go out and do it on your own." Next day, Troy spent $50 to get a business license and soon found 12 local business customers. Even though these customers had nothing to do with the family business, his father wasn't pleased and promptly fired him. (Although it wasn't all that funny at the time, they now laugh about this.)

Today, Layer 9 serves a wide range of industries, including medical, legal, financial and construction. Their goal is to ensure technology is always there and ready to support your core business initiatives without creating headaches and interruptions. They accomplish this through the focused application of industry best practices such as Cybersecurity Maturity Model Certification, monthly site visits and 24/7 monitoring.

The increasing shift toward industry-standard security protocols such as CMMC has prompted a change in the way Layer 9 supports its clients. Information management, security and business operations now require a much tighter integration to effectively align technology with business needs and goals. This goes far beyond simply stringing cables and plugging in servers. Today, Layer 9 works alongside their customers in a partnership to ensure information gets managed effectively, securely and in a way that moves the business forward.

People ask, "Where did you come up with the name Layer 9?" It refers to the seven layers within the Open Systems Interconnection protocol used to describe how your computer communicates with your network. The eighth layer represents the end user who enters information into the computer.

Layer 9 represents Troy and his team, jointly responsible for bringing everything together for your business in a way that's effective and secure.

Troy has a number of technical certifications, most recently Certified Ethical Hacking because he wanted the most current information on the strategies "bad actors" use to infiltrate business networks, along with the tools they use.

Troy loves getting up every morning – it's another opportunity to learn something new and help someone out by protecting them from the things they don't want to happen.

Troy and his wife got married at 21, started a company at 22, and started having children at 23. Today they have one daughter and one son, both in their teens, and as a family they love spending time together outdoors – hiking, snowboarding, wake-surfing, and anything involving a lake and a boat.

To contact Layer 9, Suffolk, VA 23435:
- Web: https://www.layer9it.com
- Email: tmccollum@layer9it.com
- Phone: 757-598-3439

CHAPTER 19

WHAT LEVEL OF CMMC 2.0 COMPLIANCE IS RIGHT FOR YOUR BUSINESS?

BY WAYNE HUNTER,
President & CEO – AvTek Solutions, Inc.

On January 31, 2020, new regulations were introduced that dramatically change the way Department of Defense contractors and subcontractors do business with the DoD. That was the day the US Office of the Under Secretary of Defense for Acquisition and Sustainment (OUSD (A&S)) released Cybersecurity Maturity Model Certification 1.0.

CMMC 1.0 consisted of five levels:

- Level 1 is Basic Cyber Hygiene
- Level 2 is Intermediate Cyber Controls
- Level 3 is Adequate (or Good) Cyber Controls
- Level 4 is Proactive Cyber Controls
- Level 5 is Advanced Practices

The goal of CMMC 1.0 was to safeguard and regulate Controlled Unclassified Information (CUI). While it was a good starting point, many in the industry felt there was room for improvement. For example, it called for DoD contractors and subcontractors to be subject to third-party assessments of their cybersecurity procedures, regardless of their role and the sensitivity of the information they handled. This requirement created a huge backlog at the CMMC Third-Party Assessor Organizations (C3PAOs), which are designated to assess whether companies have met the requirements. Another issue was that CMMC 1.0 priced out smaller firms from bidding on contracts because of the rigorous assessment process.

The OUSD received and evaluated feedback from the Organizations Seeking Certification (OSCs), Congress, C3PAOs and other stakeholders. This feedback fueled improvements to make things simpler, reduce costs (particularly for small businesses), increase trust in the CMMC assessment ecosystem and, according to the Acquisition & Sustainment website (acq. osd.mil/cmmc/faq.html), "[clarify and align] cybersecurity requirements to other federal requirements and commonly accepted standards."

CMMC 2.0 RELEASED

The result was CMMC 2.0, released in November 2021. The most obvious improvement was a reduction in the number of levels from five to three. They essentially eliminated Level 2 (rolling it into Level 1) and Level 4 (rolling it into Level 5).

The new CMMC 2.0 levels are:

- Level 1 – Foundational
- Level 2 – Advanced
- Level 3 – Expert

(It's important to note that CMMC 1.0 is not a certification that has to be achieved before moving on to CMMC 2.0. CMMC 1.0 has been replaced by CMMC 2.0.)

Another notable difference is that CMMC 1.0 did not allow the use of Plan of Action and Milestones instead of passing a CMMC third-party assessment where the full set of requirements were met. A POA&M highlights the specific measures a company needs to take to eliminate deficiencies. In CMMC 2.0, a POA&M can be submitted to extend the final implementation of unmet practices—*for a maximum of six months beyond the initial third-party assessment.* This would apply to a very limited subset of noncritical security controls.

This move to the CMMC 2.0 model is great news for OSCs because it streamlines the process and makes it easier to understand what level of CMMC 2.0 certification a company needs to achieve to do business with the DoD. Plus, it brings clarity to the processes and controls which businesses are required to implement to safeguard their data from cybersecurity hackers looking to inflict damage upon their company and the US government.

What follows is the information necessary to determine what level of CMMC 2.0 compliance you need for your business...

CMMC 2.0 LEVEL 1 – FOUNDATIONAL

The first question to ask yourself is "Do I have a contract with the government?" If the answer is "Yes," you likely need to become Level 1 certified because you have what's referred to as Federal Contract Information (FCI). FCI is not information intended for public release. It is information provided by or generated for the government under a contract to develop a product or service for the government. Examples of FCI are any emails transmitted from the DoD to the defense contractor (and vice versa), any other subcontracts and policies needed by the defense contractor and any information that has been garnered as a result of instant messaging, video conferencing, etc. CMMC Level 1 will not apply to some FCI commonly known as contracts for commercial off-the-shelf products.

To become Level 1 certified, an OSC must adhere to 17 basic

practices from NIST SP 800-171r3.[1] NIST SP 800-171 refers to the National Institute of Standards and Technology Special Publication 800-171, a set of standards to be used to safeguard and distribute material that is sensitive but not classified. More information about this is provided later in the chapter.

Level 1 is a self-assessment (although you could be audited at any time). To remain Level 1 compliant, every year your business must upload a self-assessment report to the DoD. The report must be signed off by a high-level executive within the company who is accountable for the information in the report being accurate.

Even if you don't have a contract with the government, it is *strongly recommended* that you achieve a CMMC 2.0 Level 1 certification. When you do, you will be aligned with the 17 basic practices from NIST SP 800-171, which means your company will be better protected against cybersecurity hackers. When you achieve Level 1 compliance, your business will be ahead of most companies when it comes to safeguarding your data.

Although it's the starting CMMC 2.0 level, achieving Level 1 certification is by no means an overnight process. If you do everything by the book, it usually takes between six to eight weeks to achieve CMMC 2.0 Level 1 compliance.

It's estimated that, of the approximately 240,000 companies that do business with the DoD, at least 140,000 companies are going to need to be Level 1 certified.

CMMC 2.0 LEVEL 2 – ADVANCED

Your business will require CMMC Level 2 certification if you have FCI and you deal with Controlled Unclassified Information. On the Defense Counterintelligence and Security Agency website (dcsa.mil/mc/isd/cui/), CUI is defined as "government created or owned information that requires safeguarding or

---

1. NIST SP 800-171r3 is the current version as of July 2022.

dissemination NIST SP 800-171r3 is the current version as of July 2022. controls consistent with applicable laws, regulations, and government-wide policies. CUI is not classified information. It is not corporate intellectual property unless created for or included in requirements related to a government contract." On the Controlled Unclassified Information page of the Defense Counterintelligence and Security Agency website, they note that CUI is "the path of least resistance for adversaries. Loss of aggregated CUI is one of the most significant risks to national security, directly affecting lethality of our warfighters." To become CMMC Level 2 certified, an OSC must fully implement the 110 controls (referred to as "practices" in CMMC) aligned with NIST SP 800-171r3. With Level 2, you must have a C3PAO visit your business and assess whether you have met the requirements. (Whoever helps you prep for CMMC Level 2 cannot be part of the C3PAO team that performs the formal CMMC Level 2 assessment.) To maintain your Level 2 certification, a third-party assessment is required every three years.

Note: Not all businesses that deal with FCI and CUI will have to have a C3PAO assessment every three years. A small segment of FCI and CUI companies will be allowed to do annual self-assessments instead, based on the sensitivity of the data and contractual requirements. For example, a company that develops parts for a weapon system would need a C3PAO assessment, while a company that designs military uniforms or boots may not.

Once the OSC is assessed, the C3PAO submits a recommendation for Level 2 certification to the CMMC Accreditation Board. Your Supplier Performance System Score is also submitted. The CMMC AB reviews the final C3PAO report and documentation for accuracy and completeness, and the CMMC Level 2 certification is awarded to the OSC.

It's estimated that at least 80,000 companies that do business with the DoD will need Level 2 certification.

CMMC 2.0 LEVEL 3 – EXPERT

Before a company can secure Level 3 certification, it must achieve Level 2 certification. You will require Level 3 certification if you have FCI, CUI *and* Controlled Technical Information. CTI is a subset of CUI and is defined as technical information with a military or space application that is marked with a distribution statement in accordance with Department of Defense Instruction 5230.24. The definition from the National Archives website is "technical information with military or space application that is subject to controls on the access, use, reproduction, modification, performance, display, release, disclosure or dissemination."

They go on to say, "Examples of technical information include research and engineering data, engineering drawings, and associated lists, specifications, standards, process sheets, manuals, technical reports, technical orders, catalog-item identifications, data sets, studies and analyses, and related information, and computer software executable code and source code."

Unlike Level 2, where a C3PAO visits you to validate the implementation of the 110 practices, Level 3 certification is done by the Defense Industrial Base Cybersecurity Assessment Center. A government-led assessment will be conducted every three years.

To be classified as Level 3, your business must comply with the 110+ practices that are based on the NIST SP 800-171r3[2] update released in July 2022 and NIST SP 800-172A supplement update, https://doi.org/10.6028/NIST.SP.800-172A, released in March 2022. The main difference between NIST SP 800-171 and NIST SP 800-172A is that the latter provides 10 families of enhanced security requirements designed to safeguard critical infrastructure.

It's important to point out that companies that require Level 3

---

2. NIST SP 800-171r3 is the current version as of July 2022.

are not just companies that deal *directly* with a military or space application. It could be companies that, to fulfill their contract obligations, need access to military- or space-related buildings.

It's estimated that fewer than 1,000 companies that do business with the DoD will need Level 3 certification.

CMMC 2.0 AND NON-US COMPANIES

International companies that wish to supply, contract and subcontract with the DoD will be required to become CMMC 2.0 compliant. This excerpt from the CMMC FAQs page, https://www.acq.osd.mil/cmmc/faq.html, on the Acquisition & Sustainment website explains it: "The DoD intends to engage with our international partners to establish agreements related to cybersecurity and ensure that foreign companies that support U.S. warfighters will be equipped to safeguard sensitive national security information. These agreements will establish a framework to address the application of CMMC to non-U.S. companies. Implementation of such agreements will be accomplished through the rulemaking process."

CMMC 2.0 is expected to be included in some contracts as early as March 2023 and phased into all contracts within a few years. Even though that date might seem far enough away for you to have some breathing room, the time to prepare your business for certification is right now. The preparation takes time, and if your business requires a CMMC Level 2 certification performed by a C3PAO, you'll want to get in the queue as soon as possible. As of July 2022, there were only 16 approved C3PAOs for approximately 240,000 DoD contractors and subcontractors. If the number of assessors doesn't dramatically increase, it could put your business's ability to bid on DoD contracts in serious jeopardy.

Whichever level of CMMC 2.0 is appropriate for your business, you must recognize that there is no quick fix. Don't take on

CMMC 2.0 certification haphazardly, without a plan and an objective. If you do, you won't be successful. Every business must take the time to put together a detailed plan on how to secure itself from foreign invaders. When you take this seriously, your company will benefit in terms of access to contracts and increased security for your company, your clients, and the United States of America.

About Wayne

Wayne Hunter is the president and CEO of AvTek Solutions, Inc. Based in Texas, AvTek Solutions provides IT services and IT support for the financial services industry in Texas and the surrounding states. As a veteran, when the Department of Defense (DoD) announced Cybersecurity Maturity Model Certification (CMMC) back in 2020, Wayne knew AvTek had to do its part. This came as no surprise to Wayne's colleagues and customers because they know he never shies away from a challenge and is always willing to adapt to the ever-changing technology landscape. Wayne quickly put the wheels in motion for AvTek to become a CMMC Registered Provider Organization to help DoD contractors and subcontractors become CMMC compliant.

Before AvTek Solutions, Wayne spent six years in the Navy, where for two years he went through the Navy's electronic training program (one of the best training programs in the world) and then spent four years on the USS Dallas (SSN 700) submarine. After the Navy, Wayne worked for a supercomputer company in Dallas, where he noticed many businesses didn't have the technology in place to address their large-scale automated backup operation requirements. In response, he launched Lexicon Information Concepts, LLC, which, after seven years of success, he sold to one of his vendors, Legato Systems, Inc. Wayne worked for Legato Systems as a senior vice-president for a while after the acquisition but quickly realized that entrepreneurship is in his blood.

In 2004, he co-founded AvTek Solutions on the core beliefs of communication, loyalty, integrity, knowledge, and continuous growth. Wayne is a firm believer in the maxim "Good customer service shouldn't be just a department; it should be the entire company." He is committed to providing the best customer service in the business, and he and his entire staff always go the extra mile for their clients. Wayne has over 30 years of experience in information technology, focusing on implementing storage and data systems, and IT management and systems integration.

Today, AvTek Solutions is in high demand. They partner with global leaders such as Hewlett Packard, Dell Technology, and the cloud computing company VMware. AvTek grew 22% in 2020 and 33% in 2021. With their financial services marketplace booming and their CMMC compliance gaining awareness and momentum, AvTek is on track to increase revenue by 24% this year.

In the community, Wayne is a longtime supporter of the Special Olympics. He also supports his clients' community service in any way he can. For instance, Wayne partners with Austin Bank employees to help build beds for children at homeless shelters. He and his wife, Susan, have been married for 35 years. Together, they have a grown daughter who is a teacher and coach. Wayne and Susan live on a 34-acre Texas farm, where they enjoy spending time at the lake, at a Texas Rangers game or in the woods.

For more information, contact Wayne at AvTek Solutions, Inc.:
- Email: wayne.hunter@avteksolutions.com
- Phone: 214-778-2983
- Web: https://www.avteksolutions.com

CHAPTER 20

THE IMPACT OF NONCOMPLIANCE

BY WILL NOBLES,
Founder & CEO – Vector Choice Technology Solutions

Even though it happened a few years ago, I remember the call as if it had occurred yesterday. A company that had been referred to us frantically called me up. They'd just been hit with a ransomware attack, and they were looking for help. Their business involves making parts for some guns used by the US military. The phone call happened just before Cybersecurity Maturity Model Certification 1.0 (CMMC 1.0) was introduced. While they should have been compliant with National Institute of Standards and Technology Special Publication 800-171, they were nowhere near compliant. They had been more vulnerable to hackers and ransomware attackers than most home computers. To make matters worse, the last backup they had was 14 months old. Their IT department was too busy to monitor the backups.

There are two schools of thought on whether you should pay off a ransomware attacker. Some are adamant that you should not. Because when you do, the attacker knows you are willing to pay off a ransomware money request and your business will become a high-priority target for the cybercriminals in the future. However, in some cases, it makes sense, especially if you essentially have to start from scratch with your data and the amount you have to pay out is minimal when compared to the overall costs of the loss of data and downtime and the loss of revenue (and potential fines) that occur as a result.

So, after weighing the pros and cons with my new client, we decided that the most cost-effective solution would be to pay the ransomware. The ransomware attackers insisted on being paid in Bitcoin so the money couldn't be traced. While it's easier to transfer money to Bitcoin today, I found myself standing in front of a Bitcoin ATM feeding $100 bills into it until the total was $60,000. The money was transferred, and my new client's data and business were restored. While ransomware attackers may not be ethical, they are logical. They understand that if they don't restore a business's data after an attack, future businesses that fall victim to ransomware attacks will simply refuse to pay the ransom.

Ninety-four percent of malware attacks are delivered by phishing emails, according to Verizon's 2019 Data Breach Investigations Report. (A phishing email is a fraudulent email that either asks you to input sensitive information or deploys malicious software on the clicker's computer.) The same report lists the average cost of a data breach at $3.62 million, with about 60% of small businesses having to close their doors forever within six months of an online attack. The more advanced ransomware can infect every device connected to the victimized computer's network. Often the malicious virus runs in the background and simply collects information for some time before the ransomware attack is initiated.

When bigger organizations get compromised through a ransomware attack, it's understood that, in the name of transparency, they inform the public that they've been hacked. However, even though they should, often when a smaller organization is the victim of a ransomware attack, they keep it on the down-low. They know that if they inform the public about it, their reputation will take a colossal hit and they could lose a large part of their clientele. That was the case with the company that paid $60,000 to get their data and business restored. (I played no role in their decision not to inform the public.) Having said that, if the government finds out they were hit with a ransomware attack because of sloppy practices, the fine will be much greater than if they had been up-front about being attacked.

When it comes to CMMC 2.0 compliance, approximately 65% of my clients are eager to do the right thing and take the necessary steps to become compliant. If you were to apply that ratio to the approximately 240,000 companies that benefit from the hundreds of billions of dollars of defense spending (keeping in mind that the 65% number is an estimate and not based on scientific data), that would leave 84,000 who aren't quite sure they need to become CMMC compliant.

This highlights the first impact of noncompliance: It's a *huge business opportunity* for the 195,000 (or whatever the number may be) businesses that are committed to becoming CMMC 2.0 compliant as soon as possible.

So why wouldn't a business become CMMC 2.0 compliant? There are several reasons. The first is their attitude toward the government. Some people distrust the government and view CMMC 2.0 as "just another cash grab" and "more unnecessary regulations." There are a number of ways that having that type of lackadaisical attitude toward CMMC 2.0 compliance could impact your business. Here are the top six...

1. **Loss of contracts**. In 2022, the United States Department of Defense's discretionary budget was $715 billion. The 2023 budget is $773 billion. In the not-too-distant future, if you're not CMMC 2.0 compliant, you won't be able to bid on (or renew) any contracts from the DoD. If your business only does business with the DoD or a substantial amount of your revenue comes from DoD contracts, this could lead to your company being stretched to the limit financially.

2. **You will suffer from a ransomware attack**. Ransomware attacks are on the rise. According to *Cybersecurity Ventures*, in 2021, a ransomware attack occurred every 11 seconds, and they predict that by 2031 a ransomware attack will occur every two seconds and cost its victims $265 billion (compared to about $21 billion in 2021). These are scary figures and a sobering reminder that businesses need to protect themselves (and the United States military) by becoming CMMC 2.0 compliant ASAP. A 2021 ransomware attack that made the headlines was the attack on the Colonial Pipeline, which disrupted gas supplies along the East Coast of the United States. A group called "the DarkSide gang" demanded $4.4 million in Bitcoin. The ransom was paid (the FBI was able to recover $2.3 million of the ransom money), but the government determined that Colonial Pipeline's cybersecurity measures were not up to par and the attack might have been prevented had stronger protections been in place. As well as criminal networks, these attacks are carried out by Russian (the DarkSide gang is thought to be a Russian-based criminal organization) or Chinese groups under the blessings of their respective governments. Plus, there is now something called Ransomware-as-a-Service. A ransomware author makes their software available to "affiliates." These affiliates, who often possess little technical skill, use the software to hold people's data hostage while demanding ransomware (paying a percentage of their take to the author).

3. **You'll go out of business**. Ransomware groups are becoming greedier and greedier. The average ransomware payment in 2021 was $570,000 (up from $312,000 in 2020), according to the Unit 42 security consulting group. Few companies can withstand a financial hit like that when combined with the downtime, loss of revenue and terrible reputation that goes with it. According to the National Cyber Security Alliance, 60% of small and midsize businesses that are hacked go out of business within six months.

4. **Loss of reputation**. Being hit by a cyber-attack can have a major impact on your business. A study by the Radware software company revealed that 43% of study participants experience negative customer experiences and reputation loss after a successful cyber-attack. A Ping Identity survey found that 36% of respondents would stop engaging with a brand altogether if the brand experienced a breach.

5. **You could become uninsurable**. The global cybersecurity insurance market is expected to reach $26.24 billion by 2028, up from $8.32 billion in 2021, according to Vantage Market Research. Businesses that have experienced one or more data breaches will either be looking at higher rates for insurance or discover that no insurance company will even agree to insure them.

6. **Increased likelihood that you could be fined**. In October 2021, the United States Department of Justice (DOJ) announced its new Civil Cyber-Fraud Initiative, whose mandate is to hold accountable businesses (or individuals) that put sensitive US information at risk. The plan is to use the False Claims Act to hold people accountable who knowingly provide deficient cybersecurity products and services, knowingly misrepresent their cybersecurity practices or protocols, or knowingly violate obligations to monitor and report cybersecurity incidents and breaches. Deputy Attorney General Lisa Monica stated that the DOJ "will use our civil enforcement tools to pursue companies, those who are government contractors who receive federal funds when they fail to follow required cybersecurity standards." The key takeaway is that if you can show that your business was putting in the time and effort to comply with the CMMC 2.0 requirements, you will not be subjected to the same severity of penalty as a company that has misrepresented its status and/or made little effort to be compliant.

Cyber-attacks threaten the success of the business you've worked so hard to build. Yes, it takes a significant amount of time, effort, planning and resources to become CMMC 2.0 compliant and maintain that compliance level. But it's worth it. Not only will you be protecting your business and client data from harm, but you'll also be doing your part to keep the United States of America safe from foreign cyber-invaders.

About Will

Will Nobles is the founder and CEO of Vector Choice Technology Solutions, which is ranked among the world's most elite Managed Services Providers, making the prestigious Inc 5000 and Channel Futures MSP 501 rankings four years running. Plus, they were voted one of the "Best and Brightest Companies to Work for in the Nation" and one of the "Best and Brightest Companies to Work for in Atlanta" for the past three years.

Although he first opened the doors to Vector Choice in 2008, Will knew early on he wanted to start and build his own technology company. In college, where he received a two-year and four-year degree in network engineering, he laid out a strategy to open his own IT firm and grow it into a multimillion-dollar company. By the time he was 25, Will was the VP of Technology at a large, 900-person mortgage company, managing a staff of 11 employees.

Will's business has grown at a blinding pace and landed him on the map as a cybersecurity expert nationwide. In the last four years alone, his company has grown $1 million year over year. His reputation as a cybersecurity expert has landed him on big stages all over the United States. He appeared in the Amazon documentary, Cyber Crime: It's Not A Question Of If, But When, and frequently appears on TV, including stations such as ABC, NBC, CBS, and FOX. The author of three books, Will is also the go-to cyber-expert on Fox 44 Baton Rouge.

Besides IT support, hosting, hardware and network protection, Vector Choice has a department dedicated to cybersecurity and compliance headed by Chief Compliance Officer Jon DePerro. Jon has over two decades in security and risk management. Previously, he served as a counterintelligence special agent who was involved in advanced security and threat management roles at the US Army Intelligence and Security Command. Jon focuses on not only helping businesses meet their Cybersecurity Maturity Model Certification requirements to protect their critical business functions, but he's also working with other MSPs to help them understand security, compliance, and risk management.

In addition to Jon, Will has assembled a stellar team that thrives in Vector

Choice's family-oriented workplace environment. They live and breathe by their five core values: 1) Do the right thing, 2) Take ownership, 3) Be versatile and agile, 4) Be respectful, and 5) Do what you say. Will says the key to success is listening to his clients and employees. He knows that listening shows respect, fosters strong relationships, and helps you understand someone's experiences and needs.

Clients trust Vector Choice because they are a client-first cybersecurity- and compliance-focused IT provider with an experienced team who love what they do and respond fast. Based out of Atlanta, GA, Vector Choice has offices in Baton Rouge, LA; New Bern, NC; Washington, DC; Mobile, AL; Philadelphia, PA; and Nashville, TN. Vector Choice serves clients in 17 states and three countries.

For more information, contact Will at Vector Choice Technology Solutions:
- Email: will@vectorchoice.com
- Phone: 877-468-1230
- Web: https://www.vectorchoice.com

CHAPTER 21

STOP DOING CMMC COMPLIANCE THE HARD WAY

BY MATT KAHLE,
President – Real IT Solutions, Inc.

Remember the famous Disney cartoon, *Beauty and the Beast*?

It's a love story, but it certainly didn't start off that way. The first time Belle met "the Beast," she was absolutely appalled at his manners and attitude. He was rough…rude…impossible to love. But as she got to know him better, over time her affections grew. His inner strength and goodness eventually came through.

There's another "Beast" out there now causing you concerns – Cybersecurity Maturity Model Certification (CMMC) – and it may seem a bit unnerving.

Now, I get it. Anytime you see an acronym – especially one created by the US Department of Defense (DoD) with regulation at its heart and soul – you probably cringe.

And even though you're hearing growing buzz about the value of embracing and implementing CMMC in your business, your first instinct is likely to head for the hills – because you probably think investing all the time, energy and effort required to put these standards to use just won't be worth it.

Well, as Belle learned, first impressions can be misleading. Because, as she eventually discovered, the "Beast" brings with it some powerful benefits as well.

THINK CMMC DOESN'T MATTER TO YOU? WELL...

The US Government requires that every vendor and contractor they do business with first clears the bar when it comes to having rigorous cybersecurity protections. Now, for any company offering services such as Software-as-a-Service applications for use by military hospitals or the VA, you would of course expect to be required to be compliant.

However, just because you're NOT dealing directly with the DoD in that manner, it doesn't let you off the hook, because if you supply goods or services used by ANY part of the defense industry, you could be responsible. And it might involve services or products about as far removed from what you'd consider "national security" as you could imagine.

For example, let's say you're in the food industry and you sell orange juice to a military base. Believe it or not, the quantity of orders you send to that base could well be considered protected information. The reason orange juice falls under this kind of scrutiny is that if you normally send 100 cases to this base and the next week you get an order for 600 cases, that information could be used to determine that the base is staffing up in preparation for military activity or some other mission. So now the number of cases of orange juice you send to a military base is considered protected information, and your whole organization needs to be certified as CMMC compliant.

And think just how many times a government regulation winds

up getting pushed down into everyday life. Cybersecurity hygiene has always been a good idea, but you can see that it's almost certainly coming soon to a manufacturer or organization affecting you.

That's why you should start thinking about CMMC. Fortunately, you don't have to reinvent the wheel – everything's clearly laid out for you on how to do things to become secure and compliant. CMMC provides you with a clearly defined framework of best practices and will open your eyes to areas you hadn't thought of before. It uncovers blind spots and forces you to address weaknesses you likely didn't know existed.

WHY EVERY BUSINESS SHOULD CARE ABOUT CMMC

Let's say you're a feisty competitor to one of the world's largest manufacturers of office furniture. You start building the very best, most comfortable office chair on the planet, and you want to make a name for yourself.

And when you hear about this CMMC stuff, you ask, "Why should I care about CMMC compliance? What's in it for me?"

This is a fair question, because achieving CMMC compliance will require an investment in time, energy, and infrastructure. And as a business owner or manager, you need to make sure you get a solid return on that investment.

Let me share a couple reasons why I think it's wise to become CMMC compliant:

- First, CMMC offers an easily identifiable and recognizable set of best practices that a company can be known for following. Think about it. Along with the benefits of being able to do business with the government, by embracing CMMC you also demonstrate to the world your commitment to excellence. It's just the right thing to do.

And when you do achieve CMMC compliance, it acts as an official "Seal of Approval" that your business is operating in a way that handles vital data securely and correctly. It legitimately gives you a leg up over competitors when choosing potential companies to do business with or vendors to outsource projects to.

- Second, CMMC can also make your job easier. For example, we had one customer who asked for our help with compliance because they regularly do business with several larger organizations who all make security a priority. And when requesting bids, they sent out giant questionnaires asking for specific details on how they will be handling IT security.

They could have spent hours responding to these questionnaires by answering questions bullet point-by-bullet point, noting that "we follow this methodology here" and "we follow that methodology there." OR ... they could simply have attached their CMMC certification.

Of course, you'll have to make an initial investment in time up-front to make sure you get that certification, but there's a huge savings in time and energy later when doing these kinds of proposals.

Having that certification in place just puts you a step ahead of everybody else.

THE KEY CHALLENGE OF IMPLEMENTATION ISN'T TECHNICAL

The technologies necessary to ensure CMMC compliance are very well established and documented, but when you start looking into CMMC, it's easy to get overwhelmed.

There's a lot of highly technical jargon involved with CMMC that affects practically every aspect of your business – physical infrastructure, auditing, media protection, recovery, training, and more. And when you have to consider the breadth of the departments, systems and personnel involved – each requiring assessment and consideration – the whole process can seem daunting.

But it's definitely NOT impossible. Even though there are hundreds of different options from which to choose, you don't have to feel like you need to put in place an advanced software development effort to achieve compliance.

You don't have to reinvent the wheel from the technical perspective, so getting that part of it done is not nearly as scary or expensive as you might think. It's all been done before. Instead, the main challenge of implementation depends primarily on the policies and the people involved.

And that's where most efforts fail. You must convince your team, your employees, and your organization to care about compliance. It needs to become more than just another management directive – it must become part of your entire corporate culture.

It boils down to making your team understand, care about, and take pride in the fact that your business has gone the extra mile to achieve CMMC compliance. (After all, if you've got your organization humming along and you have the framework in place, why wouldn't you and everyone else be proud of that?)

Therefore, the key challenge to overcome is getting everyone on board in creating a culture that values security and compliance. Once you get that established, it's much easier moving forward, because people are already in that frame of mind.

IT'S EASIER THAN YOU THINK AND COULD MAKE A HUGE DIFFERENCE

Putting CMMC to use in your business is easier than you might think, and that's key.

You need to adjust your mindset about CMMC – it's not just this big stick that someone's going to use to beat your cybersecurity processes and systems into shape. Instead, it's more accurately viewed as an opportunity to make your business shine in comparison to your competitors.

And even though compliance isn't mandatory outside of a relatively limited domain of DoD-affiliated industries, the writing is on the wall, and there's little doubt that certification is just one more thing businesses will be asked to consider over the next few years.

It's important to realize that you don't need to go through all that time and effort to learn the ins and outs of implementation all by yourself. There are companies like ours that have the experience and know-how to make it happen much more efficiently – as well as a track record of keeping businesses up and running when disasters due to less than optimal security planning DO happen.

For example, we had one customer whose security infrastructure clearly had significant problems when we came on the scene. The most glaring issue involved physical security – they had their mainframe, their servers, and their switches all just sitting in the middle of a large open room. It wasn't enclosed, it wasn't climate controlled; everything was exposed and waiting for disaster to strike.

We reminded them regularly about this, put it at the top of their list to address, but they let things slide. Then one day, a severe thunderstorm tore through the area, causing high winds that literally ripped off the roof. Rain drenched the inside of the building and took out the entire system.

Fortunately, we had gone through several stages of disaster preparedness, and by the very next day, our incident response team was able to bring them back up and running as if nothing had happened.

REMEMBER, CMMC IS NOT THE MONSTER YOU MAY HAVE ORIGINALLY IMAGINED

At my company, Real IT Solutions, we put a major focus on protecting our customers (many of them small manufacturers) from cyberthreats of all kinds. And because keeping the supply chain operational and secure has become even more mission critical to the US and its government, compliance with CMMC has become a far greater priority in the manufacturing space.

For example, we're seeing it being pushed through from tier 1 auto suppliers on down, as well as from insurance companies. And they're only the tip of the iceberg when it comes to more and more businesses driving CMMC.

Clearly, momentum's building toward wider acceptance and implementation. And again, it's not as intimidating a process as you might imagine – you simply need to make a couple of slight adjustments in mindset when it comes to how you perceive "compliance" as a concept:

- **FIRST** – Stop thinking about CMMC like it's a kind of regulatory punishment, where some government agency's going to hammer you into obedience. Instead, start seeing it as a highly effective means to reassure your customers that you take cybersecurity seriously.

  When you're CMMC compliant, you get a virtual "Stamp of Approval" that assures your customers, your vendors, and your employees that you're doing the right things to protect your products, protect your relationships with your clients, and protect your data.

- **SECOND** – Take pride in being CMMC compliant. Look – if you're doing all the right things to protect yourself and your customers from cyberthreats, why not leverage CMMC as a means to demonstrate your commitment to the process and prove it to everyone?

  Olympians train and prepare for years, and when they win, do they toss away the medal? Do they have their names stricken from the record books? Not a chance; they go through all that work to be the best and then they want to be recognized for it.

Our approach is to systematically break down the act of getting compliant into a very clear series of tasks that can be identified, tracked, and completed. Doing it in this way lets us take a shotgun approach to the different aspects of CMMC that delivers the most impact for the effort involved, enabling us to work our way through the 14 different knowledge areas as quickly as possible.

As someone who helps keep businesses secure, I can state without hesitation that CMMC makes our job easier. It helps me sleep better at night knowing my customers have gone through the process, have followed the recommendations, and are protected and ready when the next attack occurs.

So, stop thinking of compliance as this burdensome thing you're forced to submit to. Instead, start thinking of CMMC as a tool that provides you with the means to prove to the world that your business is responsible, proactive, and passionate about doing the right thing to keep its data and its customers' data secure.

It just makes sense. You're already doing most of this stuff; you might as well take that extra little step by going all in with CMMC.

About Matt

Matt Kahle started Real IT Solutions, Inc., in April 2006. Today, with the aid of co-owner Adam Peterson, it's grown to become West Michigan's highest-rated IT services company.

Serving mostly the manufacturing, architectural, engineering and construction industries, Real IT Solutions offers superior managed IT services, end-to-end network security, cloud solutions, VOIP, disaster prevention, and managed security and compliance, among other specializations.

The key reason Matt comes to work every day is simple: his passion for helping businesses achieve their goals without having to kill themselves in the process. So many businesses continually do things by taking the most difficult path possible, especially when it comes to IT and cybersecurity. In many cases, this means they may try to handle it themselves. But unless you're already an expert in this field, it can be a daunting task, as it involves reviewing the different layers of security, evaluating malware protections and firewalls, assessing training protocols for employees and so on. Or they hire a high-priced Department of Defense contractor to assist – paying outrageous prices simply because they don't know the alternatives.

Honestly, if you were to attempt to do that on your own, it would be incredibly difficult, especially if the motivation for doing so was in response to a recent cyber-attack, where you're already running scared. Instead, Real IT Solutions can come in and handle all this in a way that makes the entire process understandable and easy. Handing these tasks off to Matt's team enables you as the business owner to focus instead on what makes your business succeed.

It's all part of the comprehensive service Real IT provides.

Matt strongly believes that going the extra mile to ensure your company remains secure means more than just making sure you've checked the right boxes off some government-mandated list. Compliance should instead be a legitimate source of pride – because if you've got your organization humming along with how it manages information, and you've got a secure framework in place, why wouldn't you be proud of that? It didn't just happen – you made it a goal. You made that investment. You've shown leadership in creating a culture focused on security and compliance.

And you've made it a reality, because you've built a business where everyone comes on board already in that frame of mind.

In 2004, Matt graduated with a BS, Management Studies and Computer Science, from the University of Maryland. He also has a CompTIA Security+ Certification and attended Grand Valley State University, focusing on English and literature. He enjoys spending time with his wife and two girls, traveling, hiking and mountain biking. Matt is a passionate reader and lifelong learner. You can often find him with his head buried in a book or scanning his Kindle.

Contact for Matt and Real IT Solutions, Inc.:
- Phone: 616-209-8900
- Email: matt@realitsolutions.com
- Web: https://www.realitsolutions.com/